Does
God
Smile?

How Do I Really Know That God
Cares Anything About Me?

Larry Shoop

Pleasant Word
PW A Division of WinePress Group

Pleasant Word (a division of WinePress Publishing, PO Box 428, Enumclaw, WA 98022) functions only as book publisher. As such, the ultimate design, content, editorial accuracy, and views expressed or implied in this work are those of the author.

Unless otherwise noted, all Scriptures are taken from the *King James Version* of the Bible.

ISBN 13: 978-1-4141-1422-4
ISBN 10: 1-4141-1422-2
Library of Congress Catalog Card Number: 2009903029

To all of the people with whom I have come in contact over the years and whose interaction has contributed to the ideas related in this book, especially my wife, Judy, and daughters, Laura and Christiana.

Contents

Introduction

Our Perception of God

WHO IS GOD? What is He really like? Suppose God was your neighbor. Would He be friendly? Would you invite Him over for a visit? Would He invite you over for dinner? If you were invited and accepted, would He put you at ease or would He make you uncomfortable? Can you know God as a personal friend?

Often our answers to these and many other questions about God are shaped by historical tradition, which may or may not be an accurate picture. If we look throughout history we find that many people and cultures have viewed God as impersonal and even tyrannical. In their view, God certainly would not be a being with whom to socialize. This god is quick to judge and harsh in delivering punishments. This view is of a god who must be appeased or placated.

This concept is seen in the ancient Babylonian religion's practice of sacrificing one's children to the fire god. (The Scriptures refer to it as passing children through the fire to the fire god Molech.[1]) Parents would do this to appease the god and keep his anger from causing problems. In some more modern but primitive cultures, the same practice occurred with people sacrificing loved ones to volcanoes to appease the spirit of the volcano. They hoped that by sacrificing what was dear to them, they could make up for anything they had done that displeased the god.

Another aspect of the ancient Babylonian religion was that an individual's good deeds were compared to his/her bad deeds. Punishments or rewards were ascribed to the individual based on the ratio and comparative impact of the good versus the bad deeds. We find an example of this Babylonian religious concept in the Scriptures.[2] A Babylonian ruler observed a disembodied man's hand writing on a wall. The ruler was understandably awed and frightened at the appearance of the hand and its inscription on the wall. The message from God to this Babylonian ruler was that God had weighed his actions and found the ruler woefully lacking in good works. God used the Babylonians' own religion to bring a message of judgment.

Fast forward a few hundred years. Greek and Roman mythology taught that all departed souls went to the underworld. There they were judged and appointed tasks to atone for their misdeeds in life. When reading the mythology of the underworld we can find various punishments that lasted forever. One poor soul had the task of pushing (rolling) a large stone to the top of a hill. Once at the top, the stone would roll down the other side, so the punished had to follow the stone down and repeat the entire process.[3]

In more recent history, the concept is carried into Charles Dickens' A Christmas Carol. In the story, the ghost Jacob Marley appeared to and had a discussion with his living former business partner, Ebenezer Scrooge. Jacob explained that because of his own unkind and stingy behavior in life, in death he witnessed evil and suffering without being able to alleviate the pain they caused. This punishment served as a constant reminder of what Jacob could have done but failed to do. He wanted to prevent Ebenezer from suffering the same fate by encouraging him to do good for others.

Across the globe, Eastern religious systems included the same idea in their concept of reincarnation. The basic tenet of reincarnation expects that people improve their conduct within each life. If the soul does not improve in its treatment of other souls (all forms of life), the reincarnated soul regresses to a lower caste—a lower human social position or even other animal life. When one improves, the soul is reincarnated to a higher caste until the epitome is reached. (The epitome differs depending on the actual religion's system.)

The Hebrew Scripture Portrayal of God

At first glance, the Hebrew Scriptures also seem to reveal a harsh and unforgiving God. We see God's judgment on Egypt with plagues that destroyed the nation.[4] We also see God's command to the Israelites to destroy all men, women, children, and animals in Jericho,[5] as well as other nations and cities in Canaan. Then there is God's judgment on the Hebrew nation itself. The people had ignored God's command to obey every precept in the law He had given. The penalty for disobedience was harsh: death, disease, and captivity.[6]

But if we look deeper, it is possible to see a compassionate and gracious God. Even in the biblical judgments, He always showed mercy. How long was God patient with Egypt? Did He not bring the plagues gradually and after each one give Egypt the chance to "change its mind"? What about those in Canaan? The knowledge of the one true God was not absent from the people; they merely chose a different object of worship. With the Hebrews themselves, God waited patiently for them to return to Him, sending prophets to let them know their sin. The people, however, ignored the messages. Still, even when God disciplined these peoples, He did not desert them. The following are notable examples of individuals and peoples God did not desert.

Abraham found grace even when he failed. He asked Sarah to hide the fact that she was his wife. He also produced a child by Hagar, his wife's maid. These actions could not be considered righteous or godly, yet God had mercy on Abraham and made him the ancestor of the Hebrew nation.[7]

David found mercy and grace in spite of his sins. He prayed for God to forgive and cleanse him and recorded the prayer in the book of Psalms.[8]

Manasseh was able to find mercy and grace when he repented (changed his mind).[9]

Elijah was comfortable enough in his relationship with God that he could ask God to take his life: "I am the only one left who loves You. You might as well let me die!" God had different plans and carefully brought Elijah around to His point of view. He did not act harshly with the prophet but carefully, to ensure that Elijah understood the message.[10]

Finally, God purposed to use the nation of Israel to fulfill His plan regardless of the apparent lack of cooperation by the people. They did fully accomplish His purpose because through the nation Israel the Messiah came to save us all.

Understand (Even Somewhat Dimly) His Will

So again we can ask, Who is God? What is He really like? What kind of neighbor would He be? Can He be a personal friend? In one of the psalms the writer indicates that God does not want to force us to do His will (unlike a horse or mule that must be controlled with a bit and a bridle). Instead, He wants us to understand His will and purpose.[11] He wants us to know Him in an intimate way. We can never know God to the same extent that He knows us; however, the better we know God, the better our relationship with Him will be and the better we will understand His purpose.

Abraham was considered a friend of God.[12] Moses talked with God face to face as a man talks with his friend.[13] It was said that David was a man after God's own heart. He wanted that close relationship with God, and God wanted that close relationship with David.[14] God wants the same for us.

It is important to study His nature and to understand some of His attributes. We must really get to know Him. To start that quest in this book, we will examine several questions that deal with various parts of the nature of God:

- ♣ What if God smiles?
- ♣ What if God teaches without harshness?
- ♣ What if God approves of me?
- ♣ What if God really loves me?
- ♣ What is God's perspective toward me?
- ♣ What does God expect of me?

Although this book cannot possibly teach all there is to know about God, answering these questions can guide us into an even deeper, richer, and more rewarding relationship with Him. That result definitely will be worth the effort.

Chapter 1

What If God Smiles?

The Significance of a Smile

WHAT IS THE most simple, single method of showing approval (or affirmation) of another person? This method of showing approval does not even require the ability to talk. It is a simple gesture. Have you guessed it yet? Of course, it is a smile! A smile is unconsciously received by most people as a token of their worth as humans.

- ♣ How does a smile make you feel?
- ♣ How do you feel when someone, even a stranger, smiles at you?
- ♣ How do you feel when someone, even a stranger, scowls or frowns at you?

A smile is not expensive or difficult to give, yet it can brighten the day of the one who receives it.

One morning, I was walking from my hotel to the office where I was doing some consulting work in Chicago. I had been away from my home for two weeks and was missing my wife and daughters. I was also struggling with some system problems in the office and needed to get them resolved. These things filled my mind as I took my walk. My mood was rather gloomy (or at least heavy) as I noticed a woman walking toward me. I had never seen her before, but we made eye contact and she flashed me a beautiful smile as she passed. Though neither of us even said good morning, that simple, kind gesture on her part lifted my spirits.

In one of the offices where I worked, there was an administrative assistant in turmoil. Her personal life was coming apart. On one particular day, I heard her phone conversations with her teenage sons, a lawyer, and some others. She cried, cursed, threatened, pled, and cried some more all in an effort to make her case. To be honest, on one hand I felt rather annoyed; her animated and emotional exchange made it difficult to concentrate on my work. On the other hand, her pleas and tears tugged at my heart. When she finished her phone conversations and was sitting at her desk crying and trembling, I gave her all I had at the moment: a peppermint and a smile. She looked up and received both—and more. She knew she had disrupted everyone's work and that we could not help but hear her outbursts, but she still felt affirmed as an individual with worth enough to be granted a smile.

What happens to people when they do not receive smiles? What do we do to our children when we withdraw smiles as a form of discipline? I have another example to share, but I hesitate to do so because I was guilty of hurting my younger daughter (and actually all of my family) without realizing what I was doing or understanding the effects.

What If God Smiles?

My first and most vivid memory of my faulty behavior was an appealing look from my daughter who was seated across the dinner table from me. She was around three years old and was learning table manners, proper use of forks and spoons, and the requirement to at least sample a little of each item on her plate. When she attempted to perform according to what she figured were the expectations, she would look up at me. If my face showed approval (a smile), she could be satisfied that she had succeeded. Unfortunately, she most often received a frown or, at best, ambivalence. Most toddlers do not possess the motor skills necessary to flawlessly execute the intricacies we deem appropriate for table manners and etiquette, and her daddy should have realized it. Instead, she received a rather steady flow of what she perceived to be disapproval of her.

This kind of "discipline" continued for a number of years and my daughter internalized, withdrew, and basically felt she could do nothing to please me. We still had good times and laughter as a family—it was not all stressful—but my daughter felt deeply that she was somehow inferior as a person, was always doing something wrong, and could not please her daddy. A few times I tried to assure her that she was not evil, but my lack of communicating her worth with a smile at appropriate times influenced her assessment of herself.

The Lord used my wife to hit me with the proverbial two-by-four to get my attention. With some pretty deep soul searching and introspection, I was able to see for the first time what my actions were doing to my younger daughter, and to my older daughter and wife as well. The pictures and memories of times I failed in this respect became quite clear and vivid in my mind. We had a family meeting in which I apologized to all. We discussed my faulty behavior and my commitment to change. At that point the healing process began in my daughter. I'm so grateful that children are

3

resilient and can bounce back. My daughter has rebounded well, although it was not an immediate reversal—it took time. My change has taken time, too, and continues to this day. This time of trial for my family certainly allowed me to experience the power of a smile, or lack thereof.

A Smiling God?

If we can understand this from a social perspective, smiles for our children and smiles for other people, what about God? Does He smile? There are some who argue that God is a Spirit and therefore cannot smile. But a smile that we see, the physical, is merely the manifestation of what is in the spirit. If my spirit (my inner being, my essence) is depressed or angry, I cannot generate an authentic, heartfelt smile. The smile comes from the spirit; it is just manifested by the physical.

How can we know whether God smiles? To get an in-depth look at God's attitude we need to look closely at Jesus, the personification of God on earth. What was He like? Did He ever smile? The Scriptures never directly state that Jesus smiled. They do record one time He cried. They also recorded a few times that He was angry. To determine if He smiled, we need to look at other indicators, such as His attitude and association with women and children, His ability to handle hostile attitudes and trick questions from the religious leaders, His handling of "sinners," and His demeanor toward His disciples when they were not behaving as we would expect.

Jesus with Women and Children

What was Jesus' attitude toward women and children? The gospel writers indicate that women brought their

4

children to be touched by Him.[1] In two of the gospel references we find that at least one young child was with Jesus
and the disciples, so we can assume the mother was there
also. Have you ever known a child to want to be around
someone with a perpetual frown? What about someone with
a sour attitude? Would a mother want to bring her children
to one who always had a look of disapproval? I think we
can make a reasonable assumption from this that Jesus at
least had an agreeable disposition.

Think about this: Jesus had time for women and
children. To those of us living in western society that might
not seem to be a big deal, but in the culture in which Jesus
lived, women and children were not considered of much
worth. Even today in some areas of our world women are
relegated to the position of a commodity to be used by men.
Jesus had not bought into the culture; instead, He cared
even about those who were not considered important. They
were important to Him, as we can infer by what is recorded
about Him.

So children seemed to love Him, and their mothers
seemed to think He was pleasant company for their children.
That is one indication that He smiled.

Jesus with the Religious Leaders

Another indication would be His method of answering
trick questions from religious leaders who had, as we like to
call it in our home, "BA" (bad attitude). The Jewish religious
leaders attempted on several occasions to ask questions
they thought Jesus would have a difficult time answering.
With each of these examples, remember that Jesus knew the
questions before they were asked, and more importantly, He
knew the motivation of those asking the questions.

5

Once, some who liked the ruler Herod in power came to Jesus and asked if they should pay taxes to Rome. Jesus understood their motivation. If He said yes, they would say He was not nationalistic and was rejecting the Jewish kingdom. If He said no, He would be a rebel against authority. They thought they had Him![2] Let me paraphrase His response:

"Anybody here have a dollar?" One was produced. (It's interesting to note that Jesus did not have one of His own.)

"Ah, good. Now, where did this come from?"

Someone answered that it came from the U.S. Treasury Department.

"Well, then, if the U.S. Treasury Department produced this and they want it back, I guess it is all right to give it back. Also, realize your life was given to you by God. What does that mean?"

I think Jesus was demonstrating a sense of humor in His response. I also think He was smiling when He gave it. There was no reason for it to be otherwise. He was not trapped or stumped by the question. He knew why they asked, and His response was absolutely correct. He could have been antagonistic in His response, but what would it prove? And had He meant to be antagonistic, His response might have been quite different.

Another group, who did not believe in a resurrection, came with a different question. They came with a story about a woman who had seven husbands, all brothers, each in succession at the death of the previous one, as the Hebrew law would allow. They asked Jesus whose wife she would be in the resurrection. These folks thought He would have no answer. It seems they had debated this question successfully with the more conservative leaders who did believe in a resurrection. Their plan to stump Him was frustrated.

Jesus explained that they did not know or understand the Scriptures or they would not have asked the question. He then explained that resurrected souls are like the angels in heaven so the woman would not be considered anyone's wife. This was a concept with which they were unfamiliar (and again showed the culture's view that a woman's only identity was that of her husband).[3] It does not appear as though Jesus was nasty or harsh in His response. He could have been quite demeaning had He chosen to be, but He was in complete control. I picture Him as relaxed and smiling during the question and in the response. There was no need to be otherwise.

Jesus with Sinners

In this next example we see how Jesus handled a question from the religious leaders, and we also see how He dealt with a person who had committed a pretty serious sin. The religious leaders brought to Jesus a woman caught in the very act of adultery. They wanted His judgment on what should be done to her. This was an offense for which the Hebrew law was quite specific—adulterers were to be put to death (stoned). Essentially, they asked Jesus, "Do we obey the law and put her to death?" Their question appeared to grieve Him; He did not answer immediately. They continued to press Him for an answer. They knew He was merciful and not one to condemn (although He alone had the ultimate authority to judge and condemn). They expected Him to answer in her defense, in which case they could accuse Him of speaking against the Hebrew law. Instead He indicated, rather quietly it seems, those who had never done anything wrong should throw the first stones at the woman. We can only imagine the thoughts going through their minds at this point. What we do know is that one by one each of the accusers left. When all of the accusers had gone, only the woman remained. Again, Jesus' actions and words seem to suggest a bit of humor. I paraphrase the discourse. He asked, "Ma'am, where are those folks who wanted to put you to death?" She answered, "I think they all went home." Jesus responded, "Well, I am not throwing stones at you. You are free to go, only please do not commit adultery anymore."[4]

He could have been extremely harsh. The woman was obviously guilty and apparently did not have the best reputation. Otherwise, how would the religious leaders know how to find her in the act of adultery? Jesus, however, treated her differently, much differently than would most of us in our churches. He did admonish her to refrain from committing adultery in the future—He was not condoning the activity—but He showed mercy and kindness to her as well. I choose to picture Him with a bit of a grin when He asked the woman where the others went. He knew. I also choose to picture Him smiling at the woman when He told her not to do it again. He would not have been smiling to show levity at her actions, but to show her kindness. She was still important and valuable to Him. How could He show that if not with a smile? I think she realized she was forgiven by her God. I think she reacted in obedience to the One who showed the kindness to her.

Jesus and His Disciples

Jesus also seemed to have a mild demeanor and sense of humor when dealing with His disciples. The disciples were in a boat on Lake Galilee, but Jesus was not with them. The wind was blowing, so the sea was rough and they were rowing hard. They saw something that scared them—a man walking toward them on the water. When they cried out in fear, the man walking on the water told them to relax and identified Himself as Jesus. Peter then challenged Him, and Jesus told Peter to come walk on the water also. When Peter started walking on the water, he became afraid and began to sink. Jesus immediately lifted Peter out of the water and asked him, "Why were you afraid?"[5]

When I read this passage, I can't help but picture Jesus smiling as He asked Peter the question. Of course He knew why Peter was afraid. How many times had Peter practiced this particular feat? Peter was a fisherman. He knew the properties and dangers of water. He also knew that water is not a substance on which humans naturally can walk. Of course, Jesus knew this also, and this is why Jesus lifted Peter out of the water and walked with him to the boat. He knew why Peter was afraid and also knew what He could do to alleviate the fear. Although He was admonishing Peter with His question, "Why were you afraid?" He could certainly smile when He asked the question and probably helped Peter smile about it as well.

Actually, Jesus admonished (corrected) His disciples a number of times. If His admonitions were harsh and meant to belittle the disciples, how many would have remained? The disciples were all volunteers; they were not slaves forced into service, nor were they paid. They left their livelihoods to follow and be taught by this Man.[6] They must have seen or felt something that gave them a desire to stay close to Him (and later even die for Him). They found something in His teaching, manner, and character that made Him worthy of their loyalty. What was it? Yes, He was the physical manifestation of their God, but they did not fully realize that truth at the beginning. Why did they follow Him in the first place? They were not coerced or offered jobs; all of them had businesses of their own. He must have shown an attitude that aroused their interest. Two initially asked, "Where do you live?" He answered, "Come and see."[7] They must have had pleasant conversation because one went back to his brother and brought him to Jesus the next day. Is it possible to talk of serious and important issues and yet still be pleasant and smile?

If Jesus had maintained a constant frown or morose attitude, the disciples would not have taken the time to get to know Him. How many of us will continue long at a paid job if we have to endure constant ridicule or work with a supervisor who cannot smile and be pleasant? These men were no different. They had enough hardship in their lives. They were looking for some hope, some enduring peace. They did not exactly know where to find it, but this Man had confidence and serenity they felt and must have seen. How does one "see" inner peace? It is only seen through the physical manifestation of that which is within. Jesus was confident. He knew who He was. He knew His mission. He was at perfect peace. That had to be physically shown by the way He presented Himself and with smiles. He taught His followers, and admonished (corrected) them, but with a pleasant disposition and attitude.

These are just a few examples in the record we have of Jesus that indicate He had a pleasing personality and attitude. I really think Jesus smiled often because it is difficult to portray these characteristics (pleasing personality and attitude) without smiling. The God of the universe knew how to communicate as a man to the individuals He created. If we enjoy receiving a smile, so did the people living and coming in contact with Jesus. He used smiles as one method of communicating His love toward them. He is no different toward us; we just cannot see the physical smile as they did.

. . . .

Chapter 2

What If God Teaches Without Harshness?

Principles of Teaching

"YOU'RE HOPELESS." "try harder, stupid!" "You can't do anything right." "You have no clue what you're doing." "Why can't you behave?" Do any of these phrases sound familiar? Many of us have had teachers, coaches, bosses, and maybe even parents who have said variations of these phrases to us. In fact, you might even be one who uses similar phrases in an attempt to stimulate better performance or behavior in another. Have you ever stopped to ask yourself if a teacher or trainer must be harsh to get his or her point across? How do we define harshness anyway? Here are a few examples:

- ♣ A punishment more severe than the behavior warrants
- ♣ Personal attacks used to correct an error in judgment

- ♣ Public humiliation of a person for an error in judgment or behavior
- ♣ Constant disapproval of one's efforts as an attempt to obtain better performance
- ♣ Joy in response to another's failure

You probably have experienced one or more of these examples and can think of others as well. We do not normally forget harsh lessons we learn, nor do we forget harsh teachers, coaches, bosses, or parents. And yet harshness does not generate our best efforts. Think about those who benefited you the most and who enabled you to perform your best. In sports venues, do we learn the most and perform our best for harsh and demeaning coaches? In the workplace, do we perform our best with a sharp-tongued supervisor? In the home, do we perform our best for parents who are always critical? Can we be corrected without harshness? Can our efforts be praised even though our methods need correction and adjustment?

We can survive and thrive with demanding coaches, teachers, bosses, and parents. We can be held accountable to a high standard having high expectations, yet rise to meet that high standard when properly motivated. But constant criticisms and ridicule produce substandard results and leave any high expectations unmet. If we are always belittled and demeaned, always criticized, always told we have no ability, then we eventually will believe and perform accordingly. The drive, the ambition to succeed, the desire to set and meet high expectations is instilled by encouragers.

Encouragement as a Teaching Tool

My older daughter, Laura, had two piano instructors from her early childhood through her high school years.

One instructor was a man with great credentials. He graduated from a music conservatory, could play very well, and had a deep knowledge of music. But his method of teaching was belligerent. No matter how much effort and time Laura expended, he had nothing to praise in her sessions and always accused her of never practicing. My daughter soon realized she could do nothing to please this instructor.

She quit taking any music lessons for a while until my wife found another instructor. The new instructor was also well qualified and expected the same level of performance; however, Mrs. Dodd's teaching style was much different. She not only corrected mistakes but also offered encouragement and praise for effort and progress. Laura took lessons from this instructor through high school. We attribute a large part of her enjoyment of music and musical achievement in college to this teacher. The difference between the two instructors was their approach to teaching: The belligerent approach failed while the encouragement approach worked.

When my younger daughter, Christiana, started taking piano lessons, we didn't hesitate to enroll her with Mrs. Dodd. Christiana would have had an even harder time with the critical instructor because she was also struggling through the mistakes of her father, as mentioned in the preceding chapter. Mrs. Dodd's encouragement helped my daughter on many levels.

Christiana also expressed an interest in gymnastics, so she started taking lessons and later competed for a few years. When she ended the competitive participation, she and I began taking private gymnastics lessons together. Our coach, Tony, is probably one of the best coaches I have ever known. He corrected mistakes and worked with us to get our movements precise, but he also encouraged our efforts. Christiana gained the confidence to perform movements she never was able to accomplish while competing, and I just had great fun. While I could not accomplish the same physical feats as Christiana, this coach helped me accomplish some amazing things for a fifty-plus-year-old with no previous experience in gymnastics.

Putting this into perspective, I have to conclude that Christiana's music teacher and her gymnastics coach were integral parts of Christiana's growth as a musician. The confidence she gained through Tony's encouragement spilled over into the music arena and complemented her music teacher. Had Tony or the music teacher been harsh in their treatment, Christiana would not have progressed in gymnastics or music and quite possibly would not have had the confidence to compose her first musical score (a piano and flute duet that won first place for high school in the state). She needed the encouragement (and correction) of both instructors to build the confidence to push on toward the goal to finish that composition.

God's Examples

Mrs. Dodd and Tony are only two examples of encouragers from my experience. I could give many more, and I'm sure these stories have brought up memories of coaches, teachers, or supervisors in your life who have encouraged and motivated you as well. Now let's take a look at God's method of teaching and leading to see if He is an encourager or one who belittles and demeans.

Jesus and Peter

Peter had enough faith to walk on water with Jesus. Peter proclaimed that Jesus was the Christ of God (the Messiah).[1] Yet Peter later denied that he even knew Jesus.[2] However,

in spite of his betrayal, after His resurrection Jesus assured
Peter of His forgiveness.[3] We have no scriptural record that
Jesus chided Peter for his denial. Jesus easily could have
made an example of Peter in front of the other followers.
He could have belittled Peter in an effort to "put the fear of
God" into the other followers. But Jesus knew the followers
just as He knows our weaknesses and motivations. He chose
not to make a public example of Peter's failure.

Peter was later well able to "perform." He preached the
main message on the day of Pentecost, leading approximately three thousand people to believe on Jesus as Savior.[4]
Peter healed a lame man who lay in front of the temple.[5]
He raised a woman from the dead.[6] He was the first of the
Jewish apostles to preach to the Gentiles.[7] God was able
to use Peter in mighty ways regardless of his weaknesses
and past failures. Jesus understood how to motivate Peter
to do his best.

Jesus and Paul

Paul spent some time persecuting Christians, even to
the point of having them imprisoned and killed.[8] Why? He
was passionate about condemning this new sect (Christians)
as heresy. Then Jesus made a special appearance to Paul
while Paul was traveling to imprison more Christians. The
special appearance brought a strong message to Paul; Jesus
said it was hard for Paul to resist Him.[9] This indicates that
Jesus had taken the time to work on Paul even before He
appeared to Paul – before Paul realized who Jesus was. Was
this harshness or mercy?

Paul realized it was mercy and God's grace. We find
reference to God's mercy all through Paul's writings,
including his statements to Timothy that Paul was chief
of sinners, but that Christ Jesus came into the world to

save sinners.[10] God was not harsh toward Paul. Paul was corrected, but in the loving manner that only our God can fully demonstrate.

Jesus and the Disciples

Peter and Paul were not the only followers of Christ who received correction. One day while with Jesus, His disciples were arguing about who was the greatest. Of course, they all wanted to be the greatest; they were no different than we are. But instead of being quick to correct them by openly exposing their pride and arrogance, Jesus put a child in the middle of the fray and told them they must be like the child.[11] On another occasion He told them that the greatest among them should serve (or "is the one who serves") the others.[12] This was (and still is) a completely foreign concept to us. They, and we, want others to serve us. Jesus destroyed that concept and taught something completely different. He Himself set the example when He served them at the Passover and washed their feet.[13] Notice that He taught these lessons of humility and greatness by example, not with harsh corrections or lecture. This is a hard lesson for us (at least for me) to learn. Jesus was not harsh in teaching the lessons His followers needed to learn.

Jesus and John the Baptist

John the Baptist was in prison and knew about Jesus. Yet at that point in his life, he saw nothing great happening, politically speaking, and was beginning to doubt that Jesus was the Messiah. He sent some of his followers to ask Jesus if He really was the Messiah or if another was to come.[14] Now, John had testified that Jesus was the Messiah when John baptized Jesus. John was instrumental in directing some of his early listeners to follow Jesus when John spoke of Him as the Lamb of God. For John to ask these questions, to have doubt, would have been disconcerting to some leaders.

Jesus, however, was very kind. He could have sent a message to John indicating that John should not question what he knew and had testified to being true. John deserved a strong rebuke for such doubt. Instead, Jesus told John's followers just to let John know what was happening. They saw the miracles and heard Him speak the gospel to those in need. Jesus also gave a glowing testimony (or epitaph) of John after John's disciples received their answer. This was merely a gentle reminder to John. I would guess John went to his death in peace, knowing he had proclaimed the truth about Jesus.

Could Jesus have been harsh? Yes. Was He? It does not appear so. Why not? He understood John and his need. After John was executed, to whom did John's disciples come? They came to the One who spoke kindly to them and commended the one they had been serving.[15] Had Jesus been harsh and condemning, they would not have come to Him.

Jesus spent approximately three and a half years teaching the disciples. He spent the last six months explaining over and over exactly what was going to happen in Jerusalem—that He would be killed but would rise from the dead after three days.[16] His disciples did not comprehend His message; they did not "get it." They were clueless. When Jesus was arrested, all the disciples ran. Not one stood with Him.[17] Yet when He arose from death and reunited with the disciples, was He harsh with them? "You cowards! You just ran off and left Me to face My trial and death alone. You are not worthy of My attention or care!" He could have said those things, but instead He explained the Scriptures to them—again.[18] He let them realize who He was. He did

17

not attempt to shame or belittle them. He understood them (and us).

Jesus and "Sinners"

So Jesus does not appear to have been extremely critical or condescending toward those who were His close friends and other followers. How did He treat those not so close and those who committed "grievous" sins? How did Jesus treat sinners? Sin is reprehensible. Sin is ugly. Sin is bad. Sin destroys people. Jesus, as the manifestation of a holy God, could not merely overlook sin. Do sinners like to be told they are doing reprehensible things? None of us really likes correction, and we certainly do not want someone to openly expose our faults or sins. However, those with faults and sins came willingly to Jesus. Why? Is it because He was forgiving and kind?

The Scriptures give many examples of sinners who came to Jesus.[19] Prostitutes came to Jesus.[20] Tax collectors came to Jesus.[21] (Remember, Roman tax collectors were not like our modern-day IRS agents. Tax collecting was a coveted position among many because Rome would look the other way when the collectors charged the people too much tax and pocketed the overcharge.) Jesus did not condone their sin, yet He was not harsh in His treatment of them. Contrast His response with that of the religious leaders. The religious leaders were certainly harsh and had nothing to do with such "sinners." In fact, they considered it shameful even to be seen with them. Jesus, on the other hand, treated them with mercy and grace. He treated them with kindness, not harshness. To whom were Jesus' most harsh statements directed? They were directed to the religious leaders who did not count themselves as sinners.

What If God Teaches Without Harshness?

The religious leaders disdainfully reproached and accused Jesus of associating with sinners.[22] The accusations were true. Jesus gave an explanation, though He never stated that His association was wrong. Jesus explained to the religious leaders God's treatment of sinners. In His explanation He related three stories.[23]

The first story was about a shepherd who cared for one hundred sheep. He noticed one was missing, so he ensured the safety of the ninety-nine and went looking for the one that was lost. He found the lost sheep and carried it back to the pen containing the others. Jesus said there was more joy in heaven over one sinner repenting than over the ninety-nine who did not need to repent.

His second story was similar. A woman had ten coins and lost one in her house. She searched diligently and desperately to find the coin. The woman rejoiced and celebrated with her friends when she found the lost coin. Jesus related the story to the fact that the angels of God rejoice when one sinner repents.

His last story is the one we know as the prodigal son. Jesus told this story to show God's attitude toward the wayward child and to demonstrate the contrasting attitude shown by the religious leaders.

A man had two sons. When the boys were grown the younger son demanded his inheritance from his father. It was customary for the largest share and the most productive land to be given to the oldest son, so this younger son just wanted his share of the money so he could get off the farm. When he left, he went to a city where he had a great time spending the money. He was one of the early "jet setters" and "party animals." Then his money ran out. He got so desperate for a place to stay and food to eat he hired on as a hog farmer's helper (remember, he knew farming). When he got desperate enough to eat the hogs' food, he realized that he had made a mistake and also remembered that his father's farm workers had decent food and a place to sleep. He decided to go home and ask if he could be a hired hand.

As the son approached home, the father recognized him and was overjoyed. Note the method he used in teaching his son: instead of berating the younger son, the father greeted him with open arms and a welcome the son was not expecting. The father even threw a party in celebration. The older brother was not happy about his father's reception of the younger son and complained. When the father explained the reason for the celebration, the older brother responded harshly, "He devoured the money you gave paying for prostitutes, yet you celebrate his return." The father expressed mercy even toward this older son's attitude. "All I have is yours. But it is right for us to celebrate, because your brother was dead and is now alive. He was lost, but is now found."

If we listen to how Jesus portrayed the father in the story of the prodigal son, we'll gain a great insight. God is not saying, "It is about time you repented and came to your senses. It is almost too late; I cannot do much with you now. How brain dead you were!" Instead, God says, "How great to see you. I am so glad you came. You are *My* child and will be treated as such, with honor and dignity." The son was forgiven, and so are we when we come to Him.

This story illustrated Jesus' attitude toward sinners and the religious leaders. Jesus was letting the religious leaders know that they, like the older brother, were not responding to repentant sinners as God does. He really wanted the religious leaders to realize their own need for forgiveness and gently exposed them to the contrast between their attitude and God's. He wanted them to understand God's mercy. He could have been very harsh with them. Instead,

He exposed their attitude in the story to point out where it was wrong. He was still "calling" to them.

God and Adam

One of the best examples of God's method of teaching and His mildness in correcting us can be found in the story of Adam's transgression.[24]

Take a close look at God's reaction to Adam's sin. Adam acted in direct defiance of God's command. Did God come stomping into the garden to confront Adam? Not according to the Scriptures. In fact, God called to Adam to walk with Him as was their custom, even though He knew where and why Adam was hiding. "Adam, where are you? It is time for our walk," God called. Adam responded that he was naked. God then asked, "Who told you that you were naked? Did you eat fruit from the tree I asked you not to eat from?" God confronted Adam's sin, but do we get a sense that He is being harsh?

God had a right to be harsh. When Adam disobeyed, he opened the door to sin for the entire human family. This was not some little affair; it has had major consequences even for us this many years and generations later. Adam would now learn about work, sweat, and pain. We would continue the work, sweat, and pain. Adam would no longer have as close a relationship and fellowship with God because of his own sinful nature. Our fellowship with God would also be broken. Humankind would now war, kill, and die. God understood these consequences. As God saw Adam that evening in the garden, did He also see Adam's descendants and their cruelty and bloodshed over many generations? Yet when God asked the question in the garden, He did so not out of harshness, but of grief.

21

If harshness were God's method, He would have made demands of Adam. "Here is what you must do to make it up to Me!" would have been the response. He instead asked Adam about his sin and explained to Adam the gravity of his actions and what those actions would cost. God then introduced a method to bring God and people back together: God took upon Himself the responsibility to pay for Adam's sin. While Adam's sin did cost him, God would do all the work and make the sacrifice (the death and resurrection of Jesus Christ) necessary to repair the damage. If God were harsh, Adam (and all of us) would have been required to do the work to repair the damage.

A few years ago my appendix ruptured, but I had no idea the situation was serious. I knew I had some moderate pain, but I couldn't imagine the cause and figured it would go away in a few days. Four days later a surgeon removed my appendix and did his best to clean up the infection that had spread in my body. I spent a week in the hospital, ate nothing but ice chips for several days, and lost twenty pounds. The surgeon told my wife he had done all he could do; they just had to wait to see if I would survive. I am happy to say that I did survive, though not because of my decisions. No, my decisions almost cost my life.

A few weeks after the surgery, I had a follow-up appointment with the surgeon. I complained to him that I could not do much of anything without becoming extremely tired. At that point he had a "heart to heart" talk with me to explain the seriousness of my condition: I had almost died, and I would not fully recover for six to twelve months—and even then I could face some lifelong consequences. His straightforward words helped me realize for the first time the magnitude of the problem.

Now, how does that story relate to Adam's sin and God's response? The surgeon was not being harsh in his explanation to me. He was showing me the details of what happened in my body and the consequences of not taking action the day I first felt pain. God explained the magnitude of the sin to Adam and the consequences for the entire human race. God was not being harsh in the explanation, just factual. The major difference between the surgeon and God is that God had the plan in place to bring humanity back to a relationship with Him. God set the plan in motion to bring about the reconciliation. In Adam's case, God orchestrated the healing (reconciliation) and performed the work of reconciliation without expecting or depending on the man (Adam) to carry it out or follow through. In my case, the surgeon did his best and just had to hope I lived through it without severe effects.

God is not a harsh teacher. He knows exactly what we need when we need it. He knows when drastic action is required, and He knows when we need only an encouraging word to keep us moving in the right direction. We can count on Him to be a gentle Shepherd and Guide.

. . . .

Chapter 3

What If God Approves of Me?

The Concept of Approval

IN WEBSTER'S DICTIONARY[1], the definition of the word "approval" includes the following:

- ♣ To have or express a favorable opinion of
- ♣ To accept as satisfactory
- ♣ To take a favorable view of
- ♣ To give formal or official sanction to (ratify)

When asking the question, "What if God approves of me?" the question could be restated as, "What if God has a favorable opinion of me?" or "What if God accepts me as satisfactory?" Do we as individuals have worth or value to God? Does He see us as having intrinsic value? Do we matter to Him? That is the question we want to explore in this chapter of this book.

What are the differences in the actions of someone who feels approved and someone who is unsure of such approval? An example of these differences comes from a story in the *Chronicles of Narnia* series by C. S. Lewis. We can contrast the differences in the character Peter from the book *Prince Caspian* in the series, and the same character in the recent movie *Prince Caspian*,[2] which was based on the book.

To give some background, the *Chronicles of Narnia* books contain many allegorical references to Jesus Christ and the Christian life. The character Aslan is the god of Narnia and is an allegorical representation of Jesus Christ. The character Peter could represent many Christians in their growth and maturation process. Peter is introduced to Aslan and begins his journey of trusting Aslan in the first book of the series, *The Lion, the Witch, and the Wardrobe*. Peter grows to spiritual maturity and trust in Aslan's approval of him during the first book. In the second book, *Prince Caspian*, Peter is called upon by Aslan to establish Caspian as the rightful king over Narnia, a position Peter held for many years in the first book. Many years have passed in Narnia between the two books, and much of Narnia has forgotten the "golden years" of Peter the High King.

In the movie, we find Peter struggling with his role, wanting to prove himself again in Narnia, failing to recognize the role and position of Caspian, and making plans without expecting or wanting assistance from Aslan. Peter competes with Caspian even though Peter's real task, the task he was called by Aslan to perform, is to establish Caspian as the king in Narnia. Peter has this struggle because he does not really know who he is. He is not confident in his position, which makes him uncomfortable with the role he is really called to perform.

C. S. Lewis gives a much different character in his book. From the outset, Peter understands his role. He accepts, and in fact relishes, his role to establish Caspian. Instead of competing against each other, Caspian and Peter have great respect for each other. Peter's determination to see that Caspian is established as the rightful king of Narnia causes him to risk his life for Caspian. Peter does not have an identity crisis because he knows who he is, and he knows his relationship with Aslan.

To simplify the difference in the two characters, one knows who he is and has to prove nothing. The other is unsure of himself and therefore must establish himself. The one has confidence in the god of Narnia (Aslan) and his relationship with that god. The other is attempting to work completely on his own without the help of Aslan. The one is able to work successfully, knowing his position and approval. The other must struggle and cause a great deal of harm and defeat before finally submitting to someone else's counsel.

The Peter of the book knew Aslan took a favorable view of him—Aslan approved of him. The Peter of the movie figured that he had to prove himself to Aslan, Caspian, the Narnians, and himself to be approved, for all to have a favorable view of him. The Peter of the movie never would fully reach the level of approval he desired. The Peter of the book felt approved from the beginning because of his trust in Aslan.

We all want to feel approved. We all want to have value. We all want to matter to someone: our parents, our spouses, our supervisors, God.

Children seek the approval of their parents. They want to know that their parents value them. This approval does not imply acceptance of all behavior. A child's behavior may need correction and modification, but the value of the child should not change for the parent. It is important for parents to maintain and demonstrate that they approve, have a favorable opinion of, and are satisfied with their child even when they must correct the child's behavior. If children don't sense that approval when they are young, they learn to reject their parents because they perceive their parents have rejected them. A child's behavior often must be corrected, but the correction must not show disapproval of the child. Parents must clearly communicate the approval and intrinsic value of the child even when disapproving of and correcting undesirable behavior.

Husbands and wives also need this same kind of approval from each other. There are often differences in the way spouses relate to each other, but the core concept is that both the husband and wife need to know that they are valued by their partner regardless of disagreements, disputes, or other issues. It is part of the commitment they made to each other when they agreed to marry. The two can work together to resolve problems and handle life's hardships as they occur and still maintain an attitude of "approval" toward each other by communicating the sense of worth and value of each other.

It is normal for us to seek approval from others and for others to seek approval from us. The question is: on what is this approval based? Is this approval based on performance or something even more important? Children need to know that they matter, have worth, and are approved just because they exist. Husbands and wives need to know they are approved and have worth or value to their spouse, even when troubles, setbacks, sicknesses, or other hardships occur.

Employers demonstrate a type of approval in ways such as recognition for exemplary service, awarding additional responsibility and authority, promotions, and salary increases. An employer bases this type of demonstrated approval on value rendered to the employer. This makes sense in a performance based environment such as employment, but it is important that individuals know they have value as individuals regardless of performance. Performance may be corrected and improved with proper training and motivation; however, most people derive their sense of personal worth (sometimes referred to as self-worth) from their perception of the approval or lack thereof from other people. Once destroyed, this sense of self-worth is very difficult to repair or restore.

When people perceive they are approved—have worth regardless of performance—they can soar. They feel the liberty to take risks, to "aim high," and to fail and get back up again. The testimonies and writings of many highly successful individuals indicate that most had multiple failures from which they had to recover. Albert Einstein and Thomas Edison are two notable examples. Einstein was considered a dunce at school and was not expected to accomplish anything during his life. Edison failed multiple times before he finally succeeded at inventing the light bulb. They knew the possibility of failure. Yet their confidence allowed them to understand their worth as individuals regardless of their performance.

My daughters have my approval. They both know that my wife and I have very favorable opinions of them; they have intrinsic value. My wife and I did not (and do not) compare their performance in academics or other endeavors. We recognize them as unique individuals with unique talents and abilities. They know their value is not based on performance, and that gives them the courage and freedom to attempt, and possibly fail, without fear of losing their worth to their parents.

God's Relationship with Humans

So what does this have to do with God and our relationship to Him? Simply this: God approves of us. God has a favorable view of humans. We have worth and we have value to Him. We, the crowning glory of creation, are worth His effort, His time, and His sacrifice. If we were not, He would not give His effort, His time, or His sacrifice. God took the time to create a lovely place for us to live, took the time to create us and place us in this lovely place, spends the effort to preserve us (from ourselves mostly), has expended the effort to allow us to know Him, and made the ultimate sacrifice to pay for our sins. God bases none of this on our performance. Actually, we perform badly quite regularly, but He considers us worthy regardless.

Some people asked Jesus an important question: "What must we do to please God?"[3] They were asking, "What actions or works can I perform to be approved (found worthy) by God?" Jesus gave a very simple response: "Believe on Me!" That was such a simple requirement that most were unable to understand. The truth is, God understands His creation and He knows our capabilities and fallibility. He is not expecting us to do something to prove we are worthy of His approval. He has already given us His approval and demonstrated our worth by His own actions.

We have established the fact that we need this kind of approval. We have stated that God approves of us despite our performance. How can we know this is true? The evidence lies in scriptural accounts of God's interaction with His creation. We'll look specifically at David and Naaman, although there are many other examples.

David: Approved by God

Scripture records that David loved and worshipped God. As a young man, David wrote and sang praises to his God and continued even as he aged and incurred the responsibilities of the kingdom. The Old Testament book of Psalms contains many of David's poems and songs to the Lord. Interestingly, God promised that the Messiah would be one of David's descendants. David understood the magnitude of that blessing and even expressed to God how honored and yet unworthy he felt.[4] Yet, David lived as all men do: he failed in his behavior many times.

David apparently did not take much time to instruct and correct his children. One of his sons, Amnon, raped one of David's daughters, Amnon's half-sister. The daughter's brother, Absalom (another of David's sons), waited to see what David would do.[5] When time passed and David didn't discipline Amnon, Absalom killed Amnon. Absalom then fled the country. When he later returned, David took no action, either good or bad, toward him. Absalom must have determined David's inaction showed weakness; therefore, he attempted to overthrow David and make himself king in David's place.[6] These were very dark days for David. Apparently, the reluctance of David to correct and discipline his children gave Absalom the confidence to commit insurrection.

David not only failed as a parent, but as a husband. He committed adultery with the wife of one of his soldiers. When she became pregnant, he ordered his commander to put the woman's husband in a position where he would be sure to be killed. So when all was said and done, David committed adultery; then murder to cover the adultery.[7]

Was God pleased with David's performance? The Old Testament records and even David's own psalms[8] show God's displeasure, but they also show that God was still reaching out to David. God still honored His promises to David. David repented and God restored their relationship. David experienced consequences for his actions, but he still belonged to God and understood God's approval of him. This is great news for us to understand as well.

Naaman: Approved by God

Naaman was a Syrian army captain of great reputation; therefore, he was an enemy of the Israelites. He also had an incurable, contagious disease—leprosy.[9] In those days, people feared leprosy because the deterioration of the body was disfiguring, and debilitating, and there was no cure. Death was inevitable. Now, how could Naaman—a proclaimed enemy of the Jews and suffering from a feared and incurable disease—be approved by God? What did God do to show His approval and the worth of this individual? What effort did God take to touch this man's heart and life? How did God make Himself known to Naaman?

Possibly as part of the spoils of war, Naaman had acquired a Jewish slave girl to serve his wife. From our perspective, we can see this girl was put in Naaman's life for one major purpose: to tell him that the almighty God of the Jews could cure him, and the prophet of God in Israel could tell him how. This girl must have been exceptional. She was taken from her home, may have seen her own family and friends killed or carried away, and was forced to be a slave to an enemy of her people. Yet God put a concern and love in her heart even for her enemies, and she obviously knew something of her God and was not ashamed to boast of His power.

Naaman heard this news and saw the confidence expressed by this slave girl. Desperate to be healed, he planned to visit this prophet to obtain his cure. The king of Syria wanted Naaman healed also and donated some extra money and goods to buy this healing. Naaman eventually appeared at the prophet's door with all his stuff to pay the prophet.

The prophet Elisha was unimpressed with Naaman's high rank; he did not even come to the door (a major insult in that day). Instead, he sent his servant to tell Naaman to go bathe in the Jordan River. Naaman was not pleased with the reception or the prescription. In fact, he was a little angry. He expected the prophet to come out to him, give him some great task to perform, and cause his healing. Instead, Naaman was treated as though he were unimportant and asked to get into the dirty Jordan River.

God was still reaching out to Naaman through some of Naaman's servants whom God had prepared. They spoke softly and respectfully to him, but told him that he should try the prophet's medicine. After all, what did he have to lose? Once Naaman submitted to the prescription, he was healed—not only of his disease, but also of his pride. Back at Elisha's house, Naaman declared that he knew there was no god in all the earth except the God of Israel. He also told Elisha he would no longer offer sacrifices to any gods except the God of Israel.

God cared enough for Naaman to put some key people in his life to bring Naaman to Him, even though Naaman had performed against God rather than for Him. God put forth the effort, and Naaman received that effort. Naaman was approved by God even before he knew who God was.

Because God created us in His image and loved us before we were even born, we never can lose His approval of who we are as individuals. Though our actions may at times grieve Him or anger Him, His approval of us, His creation, remains constant and eternal.

The examples of David and Naaman indicate that God valued those two individuals. C. S. Lewis used Aslan as an allegory for God. In Lewis's story, Aslan (God) valued Peter, Peter understood his value, and Peter was able to perform. If we understand that God also values us, that God is satisfied with us, and that God has a favorable view of us, we will also be able to perform as did Peter in the allegory, and as David and Naaman did in reality.

Chapter 4

. . . .

What If God Really Loves Me?

Concept of Love

JUST EXACTLY WHAT do we mean when using the word "love"? We use the single word "love" to mean anything from mild liking to lust, to infatuation, and to deep friendship. And being "in love" may carry a slightly different connotation than choosing to love another. In the Greek language in which the New Testament was written, a different word is used for each of these connotations that all translate to "love" in English. The Greek word most commonly used to denote God's love indicates embracing a deliberate choice of the will, a commitment, to have affection for and attachment to the object of the love.[1] Interestingly, the same word is used in the Scripture where a man is commanded to love his wife as Jesus Christ loved the church.

Webster's Dictionary[2] gives one meaning of our word "love" as "to hold dear, to cherish." In this context, and in the scriptural use of the word, the word is used as a verb. It is an action word. It is something we choose to do.

Another Scripture describes the attributes of this definition of love. Paul wrote this to a group of people who had a little trouble understanding the definition.[3] I will paraphrase the attribute list as "love is" and "love is not."

Love is:	Love is not:
Patient	Envious (Jealous)
Kind	Egotistical (Arrogant)
Gentle	Selfish
Happy with truth	Happy with sin
Enduring of wrong	Quick tempered
Trusting	Quick to judge
Faithful through	Unfaithful
all difficulties	

With these definitions and attributes, one thing is obvious. The action of "love" is not based on the behavior of the object of the affection or attachment (the one being loved). It is the deliberate choice of the one doing the loving. We must remember this concept, as it has an important significance when exploring God's love for us and expressing our love in our relationships with other people.

Communicating Love

If a husband effectively communicates a full commitment to and deep affection for his wife, she will "feel" his love for her and, in most cases, will respond with love for her husband. Unless there are deep-rooted psychological issues, the wife will not take advantage of or abuse the love expressed by her husband but will respond in kind.

Conversely, if the husband *does not* effectively communicate that commitment (love) and affection, whether from ignorance or selfishness, his wife will find it much more difficult to respond to her husband.[4]

I choose to cherish my wife. I have a commitment to her, myself, my daughters, and God to have affection for, hold attachment to, and hold dear, my wife. My commitment to her, and her commitment to me, was not just for the "good" times or just for the times when we were both younger and physically more capable than we are today. We have endured a few hard experiences and had some physical challenges, but our commitment, our affection, and our attachment to each other still endures.

We have a friend whose wife developed a mental problem (some kind of dementia) at a young age. Their children were grown, but the couple was still young enough to enjoy each other's companionship. As her dementia progressed, she became quite antagonistic toward her husband and eventually caused him to leave the house. The husband was not able to live with his wife but still maintained the house, paid the bills, and did other things to take care of his wife. The woman's husband still provides for her even though she does not realize or acknowledge his care for her. He still cherishes her and has made a choice to maintain his commitment to her. He is being patient and faithful through all difficulties.

Children sometimes misbehave; however, they really want to please their parents. That desire to please one's parents seems to strengthen as a child grows, as long as the child perceives ("feels") he or she is loved by the parents. If the child does not perceive and feel that love, the child's rebelliousness and misbehavior will increase in intensity and volume. Parents have an awesome responsibility to ensure their children are loved and feel that love.[5]

It is important for us as parents to recognize the love we need to show to our children even when we work to correct behavior. The fact that a child misbehaves should never be a cause to withhold expressions of love. The child will be much better able to receive correction of behavior when the child knows and feels the commitment from the parents and still feels cherished by the parents. This kind of love is patient and gentle.

Can we find examples of this type of love being communicated in the Scriptures?

In the culture of that day (and in some cultures even today) parents arranged their children's marriages. The potential husband and wife did not always know each other before the marriage. Isaac didn't see or communicate with his wife, Rebekah, until his father's servant delivered her to him.[6] Although Isaac did not see his bride until he married her, there is no record that he mistreated her. The inference is that he chose to love her. He was committed to her.

David had a rather unpleasant experience with a local farmer named Nabal.[7] Nabal's wife, Abigail, rescued her husband from certain death by David and his army by giving them an offering of food. Abigail was dutiful and committed to her husband although he was cruel and selfish. He soon died. When David learned of Nabal's death, he sent a proposal of marriage to Abigail. Abigail must have made an impression on David when she intercepted him with her offering of food. He must have had an attraction toward her to send a proposal. In the proposal, David said he would take care of her and show affection to her. He would choose to love her and commit himself to her. She accepted the proposal and became one of David's wives.

Ruth proposed to Boaz.[8] She was a young widow taking care of her widowed mother-in-law, Naomi. Boaz knew of Ruth and made some provision to help her. She was apparently attractive and known in the community as virtuous and faithful to Naomi. It appears that Boaz was an older man and somewhat surprised and flattered by Ruth's proposal. He knew the responsibility of accepting the proposal meant that he had to take care of Ruth and Naomi. He also knew that the property he would acquire (inheritance from Naomi's husband) never would belong to his family but still would be considered property of Naomi's husband's family. In spite of these drawbacks, Boaz still chose to accept the responsibility and cherish Ruth. He showed affection for her and a commitment to her.

Demonstration of God's Love and Purpose for Individuals

Can we find some of these characteristics of love in the records of God's interaction with humans? Does God take the time to demonstrate His love even to those who have difficulty believing it?

An Israelite ruler, King Manasseh, knew what his father Hezekiah had done. His father brought revival to the kingdom by turning the hearts of the people to their God. He removed the places of idol worship and the idols. He had the temple of God cleaned up and renewed the worship of the one true God of the Hebrew people.

When Manasseh became king, he reversed all the good his father had accomplished.[9] Manasseh knew he was doing wrong, but it was easier and more pleasurable to worship the pagan gods. The Hebrew people joined in quite readily. They seemed to follow their leaders well.

Even in this case God showed His love. Manasseh was defeated and carried away captive. While a captive he repented. He realized his error and turned to God, a God who never left and still loved.

Paul, the apostle, was not always a follower of Jesus Christ. He hated Christians. In fact, he hated them so much that he attempted to imprison and execute all he could find. The Jewish leaders encouraged Paul's behavior because they also possessed the same hatred toward Christians. God, however, was still interested in Paul and took rather extreme measures to show Paul how God's love was shown in Jesus Christ. God was quite capable of destroying Paul, but instead He led Paul to Himself. God was patient and enduring with Paul. Paul received mercy and forgiveness. He experienced God's love.[10]

Nebuchadnezzar was a king of Babylon who was not known for his kindness to conquered nations. He conquered quite a number of nations, including the Hebrew nation. But God took the time to show Himself to this man who basically worshipped himself. (Nebuchadnezzar took great pride in what he determined he had built completely by his own intellect and cunning.) God corrected Nebuchadnezzar's thinking by bringing on what appears to be a period of insanity. Afterward, Nebuchadnezzar realized that he himself was subject to the rule of God.[11] God showed His love and patience even for one who had such pride and caused such sorrow for so many people.

Gideon was an unlikely general. He lived during a time when Israel was overrun by another nation that took everything of value from the Israelites. Gideon was afraid of these conquerors and was hiding to grind out his grain for food. (If they had seen him they would have taken it.) God sent an angel to Gideon's hiding place and called Gideon a great warrior. Gideon started looking around to see whom the angel was talking about, figuring it certainly could not be him. Even when God told Gideon that he would be used by God to drive the enemy out of the land, Gideon refused to believe it. God had to humor Gideon with several "miracle" signs to prove to Gideon that God was with him. Still, Gideon feared so much that God allowed Gideon to overhear a conversation in the enemy camp. There Gideon heard that even the enemy knew that he (through God) would win the battle.[12] God exercised patience with Gideon despite his doubt: Gideon experienced God's love.

What about Jesus Christ when He walked the earth? Did He demonstrate this kind of love toward others? The following paragraphs give examples of His love demonstrated in His interaction with people.

In an earlier chapter, we looked at the interaction between Jesus and the woman caught in the act of adultery.[13] She apparently was pulled from the bed and brought to Jesus by the religious leaders. They claimed to want her executed and wanted to see if Jesus would agree. We know what happened: all of the accusers went home and Jesus had a short conversation with the woman. What did He do? He did not show her disdain, scorn, or condemnation; instead, He cherished her. He showed a genuine affection for her and a commitment for her good. He never condoned or excused her activity, and admonished her not to commit adultery again; however, He still showed His affection and commitment, His love. She needed it, and He gave it.

On another occasion, as Jesus entered a village, He observed a funeral procession coming toward Him.[14] The people were mourning a young man, the only son of his mother. A widow, she had lost her beloved child, as well as her only means of support. Jesus saw the woman crying and understood her desperate need. He stopped the procession, raised the young man from the dead, and presented him to his mother. What was Jesus' motivation for performing this miracle? He simply wanted to demonstrate His affection and commitment, His love, toward this woman. He understood her need and because He cherished her, He wanted to and did meet her need. He came to demonstrate God's love.

One day, when Jesus was teaching in someone's house, a large group of people had crowded in and around the house to see and hear Him.[15] Some friends of a paralyzed man wanted to bring their friend to Jesus to be healed, but they could not get into the house. Undaunted, they climbed onto the roof, made an opening in the tiles, and lowered their friend right in front of where Jesus was teaching. The paralyzed man and his friends received exactly what they expected: Jesus healed the man and he was able to walk away. Jesus had compassion for the man's need and chose to show His love, affection, attachment, and commitment to the paralyzed man.

At another time, Jesus came near a blind beggar sitting on the side of the road.[16] The man was asking those who passed by for a little money to buy food because he could not work. He heard a crowd approaching and asked what was happening. When he learned that Jesus was coming through town, he started yelling for Jesus to heal him. Jesus took the time to hear the beggar's cry for help and restored his sight. Jesus' actions again demonstrated God's love. The action of Jesus showed God's faithfulness, His affection and His commitment to this man.

When we look at these examples of people receiving God's love we can see a change that occurs. That is sometimes referred to as repenting, sometimes as conversion. It is a change that happens because people recognize God's love. Manasseh changed while in a foreign prison. Paul changed when he came into direct contact with the Jesus Christ he was fighting. Nebuchadnezzar changed when he realized that God was more powerful than he was himself. Gideon changed when he recognized that his God could and would deliver him and his nation from slavery and occupation. The adulterous woman changed when she realized that the only One who could condemn her instead offered mercy and hope through His love. The widow most certainly had a change when she saw that her God cared enough and loved enough to provide for her. The friends of the paralyzed man saw their God show affection for them and their paralyzed friend. The blind beggar received the love of his God and realized the affection He gave.

Why Is God's Love Difficult to Accept?

Knowing what we know about God's love, we would expect people to embrace it quickly and easily. Unfortunately, hindrances exist that keep some from experiencing God's love.

"I'm Too Bad"

One hindrance is the belief that "God could never love me after what I've done; I'm too bad." I have met people who seemed genuinely convinced that was their case. But when we examine some people in the Bible for whom God demonstrated His love, we see that the magnitude of our sin makes no difference to God. Some of the saints in the Bible were guilty of some very obvious sins.

Take Paul, for example. He wrote much of the New Testament and was a student of one of the great teachers of the Jewish law. He was a member of the Jewish group called the Pharisees, who were very strict in their interpretation of and adherence to the Jewish law. We do not know for sure whether Paul saw or heard Jesus before the crucifixion; it does appear possible. We do know that he agreed with the sentence of death for Stephen, regarded as the first

Christian martyr.[17] Paul then went about finding, arresting, and condemning to death followers of Christ wherever he could find them. Paul became a murderer by consent and was vehement in his anger toward followers of Christ.[18]

God intervened in Paul's life and explained to Paul the futility of his actions. Paul immediately made a complete turnaround and became a major spokesman of the faith he had attempted to destroy.[19] God's intervention in Paul's life showed God's love for and commitment to him regardless of his past.

Peter also received God's love despite his actions. Peter appears to have been a rather impetuous sort with some very extreme behavior shifts. He was totally convinced Jesus was the Messiah and was a devout believer in God. We also see that he sometimes became afraid and showed his real human condition—weakness.

One day, after Peter and his partners fished all night without a catch (remember, this was their livelihood: no fish, no income), Jesus made a simple request. He was preaching at the shore close to where these men were cleaning and fixing their nets, and He asked if they would allow Him to preach from their boat just a little offshore. They agreed and He continued preaching from the boat. When He finished the sermon, He asked the men to take Him fishing. Peter's remarks were probably a reflection of what the others were thinking. He told Jesus they had worked all night and caught nothing (he probably also thought about the fact that he was tired and ready for sleep before the next night's work), but they reluctantly agreed to take Jesus fishing.[20]

These men understood their occupation. Fish normally find cool, deep water in which to lie during the heat of the day and come into more shallow water at night to feed. Jesus asked them to launch out into the deep water in the middle of the day to let down their nets. Now, the men did not have sophisticated mechanical devices for lowering and raising their nets. The nets were most likely shallow; they could not reach the bottom. The fish would not be close to the surface in the middle of the day. Peter was probably thinking some rather unkind things about this carpenter turned preacher who wanted to go fishing. Of course, God worked something miraculous, and they had a significant catch. So significant, in fact, that their nets could not hold all of the fish and began to break. Peter then turned to Jesus, remembering his unkind thoughts, and told Jesus that he was not worthy to be associated with one as great as Jesus. Peter understood the miracle and understood his own attitude toward the One who obviously caused the miracle.

Jesus' response is great for all of us to consider. When He told Peter, "Fear not," Jesus essentially told Peter (my paraphrase), "I knew your attitude, but just chill. That is not what is important to Me. You are! Come and go with Me."

Peter later boasted to Jesus that even if all the other disciples deserted Him, he would not. He declared he would die for Jesus before he would run.[21] Jesus knew what would happen at His arrest just a few hours after Peter's boast, and He knew Peter's desire and also Peter's weakness. We know Peter did run, then followed at a safe distance, then denied even knowing Jesus.[22] Peter *did* desert the One he vowed he never would desert. Jesus understood the weakness, forgave the weakness, and still loved the one with such weakness. Jesus, after His resurrection, sought out Peter and let Peter know he was still accepted, still loved.[23] I think that is one reason we find Peter a main spokesman of Christianity in the early church: he understood and accepted God's unconditional love toward him.

A young man named John Mark traveled with Paul and Barnabas on their first "missionary" journey. John Mark saw some pretty awesome events and really got a little scared. Traveling in that day required a good deal of work. When John Mark went home before the trip had ended, Paul and Barnabas were left to divide his share of the load.[24]

God was not finished with John Mark, nor did He quit loving him. We later find Barnabas mentoring him.[25] John Mark was able to grow and mature under Barnabas's mentoring such that Paul wrote that John Mark was profitable for the ministry.[26] It also appears that this same John Mark was Peter's secretary and wrote the Gospel of Mark based on Peter's dictation.

Job questioned God's integrity. Though he never compromised his belief in God, he did declare at one point that God was wrong to allow the calamities he had faced. He even challenged God to a debate. (How often have we felt the same way?)

God did answer Job, and they had their debate.[27] As a result, Job determined that he was wrong, not God. Job's self-righteousness was curtailed, the lesson learned, but God's love for Job never wavered. God never deserted Job (much less zapped him with lightning for expressing his thoughts) even though Job's attitude toward God was at times so malevolent.

Let's return now to David and review the sin we discussed earlier. David saw a beautiful but married woman. David sent for the woman, committed adultery with her, and then arranged for her husband to be killed in battle. This was not a pleasant scene and God was not pleased.[28]

God's love for David did not cease. God spent some time and effort bringing David to realize that his sin was reprehensible. A prophet came to David, and with an allegorical story showed David the true and heinous nature of his crime.[29] Convicted by the prophet's story, David repented. One of the byproducts of this repentance is recorded as Psalm 51, where David wrote, "Create in me a clean heart, O God, and renew a right spirit within me." The sin was grievous, yet God's love remained to bring about a true change of heart.

"God Has Let Me Down"

Another hindrance to believing God's love for us is bitterness toward God. The idea is that God has allowed too many "bad" things in an individual's life (or even in the world).

The debate about why God allows catastrophes, wars, evil men, and so forth has been raging for a long time. I certainly cannot answer that question. What we can do here, however, is examine harsh events in individual lives and see how God orchestrated the events to "grow" each person. Then perhaps we may apply this principle to our lives as well.

Jacob loved his son Joseph and treated the boy with special favors. Joseph's brothers were jealous of the preference given to their younger brother. When the opportunity came, they sold Joseph as a slave, figuring never to see him again. This was a pretty catastrophic event for Joseph. He did not expect to see his father again. And, of course, slavery was not an easy life.[30]

Joseph endured the duties of a slave and won recognition and promotions for his service to his owner. He must have decided to make the best of a bad situation. Then, when he was promoted to the highest-ranking slave position and controlled all of his owner's wealth, the owner's wife propositioned Joseph. Instead of yielding, he resisted and for his efforts won a false accusation from the woman and consequently a prison sentence.[31]

While in prison, Joseph continued to make the best of a bad situation. He eventually was placed in a position of trust, what we would call a prison trustee. We do not know how many years he spent there, but in the end, and after a remarkable chain of events, we find Joseph, the slave, given the second highest position in the land of Egypt. Joseph's story has a "happily ever after" ending, but he had to endure many hardships prior to his final promotion. It may appear that God was being cruel to Joseph to allow so much suffering in his life. But realize that God could see the "big picture" of Joseph's life and used these hardships to bring Joseph to a place where he was ready to rule. He was also ready to forgive his brothers.[32] The hard times in Joseph's life prepared him for his later tasks; they made Joseph the man God wanted him to be. Without these lessons from God, Joseph would not have succeeded as he did. Joseph's hardships allowed him to realize his success was not of his own making. He was not self-made; he was God-made.

If anyone had a valid right to accuse God, it was Job. The recorded events of his life show that everything was taken away all at once: he had accumulated wealth—it was swept away; he had ten adult children—they were killed; he had good health—he was inflicted with painful sores all over his body. All these things were taken away, and Job could not find a reason. He did, in fact, accuse God. He claimed God was wrong for allowing these catastrophes to occur.

God allowed these events to make Job a better man. Job did not realize his self-righteous attitude and pride. He had to be made to see himself from God's perspective in order to change. God used the hard events in Job's life to bring him "to the mirror." God wanted Job to realize and turn from his pride and self-righteousness. He used the events in Job's life to change him.

It is the same in our lives. God uses hard times and events in our lives to change us.

Let us return again to the example of King David. David was selected by God to become king. There was a little problem, however: Israel already had a king. David actually became a servant to the established king, Saul, and served him well. David fought in Saul's army and entertained him with music when Saul was in a bad temper. Saul had been told by the prophet Samuel that he would be replaced as king, and Saul perceived that David was the replacement. Saul attempted to have David killed by Israel's enemies; then he attempted to kill David himself.[33]

David had to flee. He and a small group of men escaped to the woods. Saul and his army came looking for David and came very close to capturing him. David continued to run and hide for his life.

David faced these circumstances and setbacks even though he had committed no crime and had served Saul well. David had killed the giant Goliath, giving Saul a great victory over his enemies. David had fought in many other battles against Saul's enemies and proved himself faithful. Although David knew he was selected as the next king, he did nothing to bring about the transition. David had opportunities to kill Saul, but did not take advantage of them. David was, in fact, loyal to the king.

David easily could have determined that life was too hard. He could have questioned God's purpose and timing. If God had chosen him as king, why didn't God just get it done quickly? But David had to persevere in hardship for many years before the final fruition of God's purpose was accomplished. God used these hardships to make David ready to be king. He also used these hardships to strengthen David's love for and dependence upon God.

Remember Paul, on whom God had mercy, even though he murdered Christians? He became a believer and began preaching. His preaching was so effective that the Jewish religious leaders, most of whom were not believers, wanted Paul killed.[34] These were his own countrymen, some had been his friends, but they did not want to hear the logical and persuasive arguments from Paul that could change their lives as Paul's life had been changed.

When Paul preached to the Gentiles he was not received any better. They did not like his message because it was contrary to their religion, traditions, and lifestyles. Paul was persecuted almost everywhere he went. He was whipped several times, stoned, and jailed all because he was telling about the One (Jesus) who had changed his life.

In Paul's travels he was shipwrecked, hungry, cold, and sometimes rather lonely. He despaired even of life at times. Yet he is the one who learned to be content regardless of the circumstances.[35] Why did he have such peace in the face of these hardships? He trusted his God and knew that God always would take care of him in every hardship, and in good times as well.

"I Don't Need God's Love"

A third hindrance to believing God loves us is the notion that we don't need God's love. The idea is basically, "So what if God loves me? What possible difference can it make for me? I can handle things on my own without God." Sometimes those who feel this way express their belief by making fun of those who do trust and depend on God. The idea is that God is necessary for the weak-willed people, but not for those who are strong and "self-made." These people must, of necessity, believe that all their talents, abilities, and opportunities came to them by their own ingenuity and efforts: "I did it all myself."

Those who consider themselves self-made generate a certain amount of pride. If one is self-made, one may easily denigrate those who have not accomplished as much, those who have not attained the same level of worldly success. Self-made individuals find distasteful the idea that God has granted us our talents and that He even orchestrates our decisions to put us in our positions.

So it was for King Nebuchadnezzar of Babylon (remember him?). Nebuchadnezzar had constructed a mighty kingdom and had an army powerful enough to conquer the major countries of the known world. All were subject to him. He built a strong city and had a splendid palace, the gardens of which are one of the wonders of the ancient world. His military strategies afforded him great conquests. He was feared and obeyed by all. Nebuchadnezzar was a self-made man.

One day as Nebuchadnezzar walked through his palatial estate, looking it all over, he boasted about the fact that he had built it all, conquered many countries, and ruled over a great kingdom because of his own great abilities.[36] Then God intervened. His statement to Nebuchadnezzar is revealing. God told Nebuchadnezzar He had brought the king to his place of power, and that God had allowed him to conquer and rule. To prove His point, God caused Nebuchadnezzar essentially to go mad. He fled his kingdom and lived in the wilderness, eating grass and acting like a wild animal. Some time later he came to his senses again and confessed that God rules even over the kingdoms of men. God then restored him to his kingdom. His testimony after this incident is recorded in the book of Daniel. He was a changed man.

Others in the Scriptures also had little regard for the love of God, but some of their stories do not end with the same change of mind as Nebuchadnezzar's. Let us take a look at Esau.[37] He was a rugged fellow, a man of the field. He provided his daily meat by hunting. He would be considered the "man's man" and was his father Isaac's favorite son. Esau had a twin brother named Jacob. Jacob was the second born, a shepherd, and not as rugged looking as his brother, but he was definitely interested in the birthright. The inheritance of God always fell to the firstborn; in this case, it was Esau's birthright.

Jacob had some soup simmering in a pot one day when Esau came in from a hunting trip. Esau was tired and hungry and asked Jacob for some of the soup. Jacob agreed, but only if Esau gave him the birthright. Esau had such a low regard for the birthright (the inheritance of God) that he consented. He counted his inheritance from God as worth no more than a bowl of soup.[38]

Judas, the one who sold Jesus to the Jewish leaders to be crucified, hanged himself when he realized the magnitude of what he had done. Judas did not understand or accept the love and forgiveness Jesus taught and demonstrated during His life. Contrast this with Peter who, out of fear, openly denied that he even knew Jesus after telling Jesus that he never would deny knowing Him. Later, Peter received the love and forgiveness offered by the One he so shamefully denied knowing. Peter recognized his need and experienced God's love and forgiveness.[39] Conversely, Judas handled his guilt on his own instead of accepting God's love and forgiveness.[40]

In one of his letters, the apostle Paul referred to the Jewish leaders, the Pharisees, as men who entrusted themselves to their own "good works." They expected God to accept them because of all they did for Him. Jesus mentioned a Pharisee who bragged to God about all his works and efforts, his fasting and prayers.[41] The Pharisees didn't think they needed the mercy, forgiveness, and even the love of God. Paul stated that those with such an attitude fall short. Their own efforts are not enough to earn God's love. In fact, no one can "earn" God's love. God freely extends His forgiveness and love to all, but those who realize they need it are the ones who receive it.

The Result

What happens when we experience and accept the love God offers? Can we be changed for the better? Can we have complete peace? Can we look at our motivations and attitudes truthfully enough to admit when they are wrong and then work to change them?

Take a look at what happened to Jonah. He was a prophet who harbored a deep animosity toward a group of people known as the Assyrians, a very cruel and barbarous people. God called Jonah to preach to the people of Nineveh, the capital of Assyria. He did not want to go mix with those people, because he also knew something about God's merciful nature. Jonah was afraid that if he preached to those evil people, God might have mercy on them and allow them to continue living. He did not want those people to repent and be forgiven; he wanted them to be destroyed.[42]

We know the rest of the story. Jonah ran in the opposite direction, but God convinced him to return in a whale of a way that Jonah could not ignore. Jonah went on to preach to those evil people and his fears were realized; they believed him and changed their behavior toward God. God had mercy on them—He did not bring destruction.

The point for Jonah was to realize his own erroneous attitude. His attitude and God's response and care for him during his disobedience are recorded in a book bearing Jonah's name. If he had not submitted to the attitude adjustment offered by God, the book probably would not have been written. The book does not present Jonah very favorably.

Ruth was a woman from Moab. The Moabites were idol worshippers, so Ruth likely learned of God from her Jewish mother-in-law, Naomi. When Naomi's husband and sons died, Ruth determined to leave her home and gods to live with Naomi and to serve Naomi's God. Ruth must have discovered something worth the change.[43]

Peter appears to have been a rather brash and impetuous person. He was the one daring enough to risk getting out of a boat to walk on the water. He was also the one who bragged to Jesus that he would never deny Him, even boasting that while all the other followers might deny and forsake Jesus, he never would do such a thing. Peter was also the one who drew a sword to keep Jesus from being arrested. He did not understand when Jesus told him to put the weapon away.

And yet, after the resurrection, Peter changed. We find him preaching and being a leader in the church, but we do not see the same arrogance. When members of the church at Jerusalem challenged him about preaching to and eating with non-Jewish folks, he did not appeal to his position or credentials (as an original disciple of Jesus). He did not claim to have greater authority and, therefore, to be above reproach. What we find instead is one who merely explained exactly what happened with the conversion of a non-Jewish household. He simply related the entire event with no defense of his actions.[44]

On another occasion, Peter came to a house where a very kind woman had recently died.[45] The people of the community were crying and recounting to him the things the woman had done and made for them. Peter sent them all out of the room. He remained with the dead woman, and God allowed him to raise the woman from the dead. Peter did not make a big show, nor is there any record of him bragging about his great act.

We know the apostle John as the apostle of love. We normally think of John as mild, even to the point of thinking of John more as a "sissy." Is that really a fair assessment of John's character? Jesus referred to both he and his brother James as the "sons of thunder."[46] James and John heard some folks telling good things about Jesus, but the folks were not in the apostolic inner circle. The two commanded them to quit. Jesus disagreed and told them to let the others speak.[47] At another time, John and James requested Jesus to allow them to "call down fire from heaven" to kill those who refused to allow Jesus to spend the night in their village. Jesus rejected the request.[48] They also desired preeminence among the disciples and went as far as convincing their mother to make the request! They wanted the most important, prestigious positions next to Jesus above the other disciples.[49]

Do these events sound like the mild apostle of love? We find later that James was killed for preaching about Jesus. John was also persecuted. We do not find either James or John striving for preeminence again. John wrote and taught about loving one another; he came to a deeper understanding of the character of his God.

We have already discussed others who experienced a behavior change such as Nebuchadnezzar, Manasseh, Paul, and the people to whom Jonah preached. What caused the change? These folks came to a clearer knowledge of God's character and love for them and made the appropriate adjustments. The changes came as a result of God's love.

God's love for us is unconditional. His love for me is not based on my beauty (or lack thereof), service for Him, or behavior. His love for you is not based on your looks, service for Him, or behavior. He simply chooses to love us because He wants to. God revealed His love for us by sending Jesus to die for our sins. Jesus himself declared that He could give no greater gift (love) than to die for His friends (us). This act of love was performed for all humans even before we knew anything of Him. We were not expecting it. His commitment to us is complete.

When we understand His love and realize that it is offered to us, it causes a change in us. Let's reflect on this on a very personal level. If you know that God has affection for you, God is attached to you, God cherishes you, and God is committed to you, what can you conclude?

- ♣ You are important to the most powerful being that exists. God is committed to your well being, and He will ensure your provision.
- ♣ You can have peace in every circumstance. Regardless of the political climate and turmoil on local, national, or worldwide levels, you have no need to fear. If economic conditions cause panic and worry, you find rest—not because your life will be perfect, but because you know that God loves you and is with you regardless.
- ♣ You can risk failure with an endeavor but remain confident that God does not consider you a failure. He will ensure that you learn and benefit from any failed endeavor, but you do not need to be crushed or disheartened. God has not dismissed you and will not belittle you.
- ♣ You can maintain confidence in God's love for you even if you fall into or yield to sin. God is willing

and able to pick you up, clean you up, and forgive you. His love does not quit.

♣ You can love and forgive others because you are loved and forgiven by God.

♣ You can risk rejection and ridicule for expressing your love to others because the God who loves you also risks and receives rejection and ridicule from others to whom He expresses His love.

♣ You will always have His love.

When we understand that God really loves us, and is really committed to us, our confidence in our position as His children allows us to shout, "Dear Daddy!" He has provided the love and forgiveness we all require. He loves me and has forgiven me and has accepted me. He loves you and has forgiven you and has accepted you. When we understand and believe the love and forgiveness that God gives, we can have true compassion on others in need because we realize the compassion and love He has toward us.

Chapter 5

· ·

How Did Jesus
Demonstrate Love at
a Well in Samaria?

O NE DAY JESUS met a woman at a well in Samaria.[1] During the discourse between Jesus and the
woman, we find that He most likely smiled at her
(at least He was pleasant), He was persuasive yet gentle in
confronting her questionable lifestyle, and He showed that
He was genuinely concerned for her spiritual welfare, while
revealing that He was the Messiah and she was important
to Him. She responded to His message and believed Him.
However, this "happy ending" did not come about without
some purposed and interesting work by Jesus before and
during the encounter.

The well was situated a little way outside the village.
The disciples had been dispatched to the village to purchase
some food while Jesus remained at the well waiting for His
"chance" meeting. The woman came to the well by herself
at a time when she expected no one else to be around. Since
that was not typical behavior (in most cases a group of
women would come to the well together), we can assume

that the woman was an outcast. Later in the conversation we discover the reason.

When the woman arrived at the well, she was not expecting to see or be greeted by anyone and was shocked to see a Jew. (She was a Samaritan. Samaritans were considered ungodly idol worshippers by the Jews of the day; therefore, most Jews avoided contact with Samaritans as much as possible and treated them with disdain when they had to communicate.) Jesus politely asked her for a drink of water. I also expect He may have smiled, but He was certainly prepared for the response from the woman. She asked Him why He was asking her for anything since she was a Samaritan and He was a Jew. Her question could have been genuine surprise that He asked anything, but it could also have been that she was looking for a reason not to comply. She had issues. She had a reputation. My guess is that her response was an attempt to push Him into saying something that would give her an excuse to refuse His request. She had an attitude problem and did not want to be nice. He was smiling and being pleasant.

Remember, He knew her mind and heart. She saw that He was a Jew and wondered why He was pleasant and even speaking to her. He responded to her question rather indirectly and was really getting to her curiosity. He indicated that if she knew who He was, she would ask Him for something to drink. She probably thought this guy was a few bricks shy of a full load, so to speak. Her response was likely a little curt as she essentially told Him He had no bucket or rope and could not get a drink for anyone. I cannot help but see Him smiling during the discourse. He then said something she could not believe or understand, but He knew it would arouse her interest. He told her if He gave her some of His water, she would never be thirsty again!

The woman quickly responded, probably with a little sarcasm, that Jesus should give her some of that water now because she got tired of having to come to the well! Jesus then addressed her moral issues, but He did so gently. (He wanted to reach this woman and was "calling" to her.)

He asked her to go get her husband. She responded that she had no husband. He must have been smiling when He agreed with her, listed the number of previous husbands she had had, and pointed out that she was currently living with a man who was not her husband. The irony is that He was right and was revealing her sin, but she did not seem to get visibly angry. If at any point He had made reference to her lifestyle in a harsh and accusing manner, she would have left. He was still being pleasant. How many people will endure having their misdeeds pointed out even in a kind way, much less with a judgmental attitude? Remember, she was most likely looking for a reason to be unkind to this man. If He had given her any reason to leave in an angry state of mind, she was ready. If He had been harsh exposing her sin, she would not have received His "living water," and she would have left in a huff.

She then conveniently changed the subject and started a discussion on where people ought to worship. She was hoping to get Jesus involved in a debate since the Jews and Samaritans disagreed about where people should worship God. Jesus responded by saying that the physical place is unimportant; God wants people to worship in spirit and truth. In an effort to show the spirituality of the Samaritans, she then indicated that they (the Samaritans) were waiting and looking for the Messiah. He was still pleasant, He was still smiling, and He told her that He was the Messiah. She experienced His behavior, His treatment of her, even His confrontation of her sin, and she believed His message. She actually returned to the village and evangelized everyone she saw. Jesus stayed a few days with these Samaritans, teaching, touching lives, and distributing His living water.

If Jesus had been harsh in exposing her sin, would she have stayed and listened to Him? He could well have used critical and demeaning words in truthfully describing her lifestyle. But His manner was much different. He was direct, but not harsh or accusing. He called. She "heard" and responded.

Jesus wanted to show her kindness; He wanted to show His love. He looked past the woman's hard exterior because He wanted to give her something better than what she had. He was patient with the woman because He chose to show her God's kind of love. She needed it, He had it, and He willingly gave it. Previously we discussed and defined that love. The example of this woman at the well is a practical example of Jesus demonstrating God's love. Jesus cherished this woman. He was committed to her. He wanted her to know that He (God) loved and cared about her. She was important to Him.

Chapter 6

· ·

What Is God's Perspective Toward Me?

IN PREVIOUS CHAPTERS we posed questions about God's characteristics to determine what God is like and if He really cares about us. We looked at examples of God's interaction with His creation and especially targeted the way Jesus Christ related to people. In this chapter we want to take a different perspective of God's dealings with humanity. We will attempt to determine God's view of us.

To do so, we will again explore facets of the life of Jesus Christ. What did He do? What did He teach? What was His purpose? In making a more detailed exploration of these questions we may begin to understand God's perspective of us.

What Did Jesus Do?

Jesus mixed and associated with the common people. Few of society's "upper crust" became close associates. Those nearest Him, the disciples, were basically laborers or craftsmen who worked to make a living. Jesus Himself was apparently a tradesman in the carpentry business until He began His preaching ministry around the age of thirty. Since Joseph (assumed by others to be His father) was a carpenter, it only would be natural that Jesus would have learned the trade and worked "in the family business."

Who were the people coming to listen to Him? Well, by the stories He told it seems pretty reasonable to assume the majority were farmers, tradesmen, and laborers themselves—with a few religious leaders scattered throughout the crowd. For the most part, though, the people who came to listen were those who wanted and needed to hear something from God. These were prostitutes, criminals, and tax collectors (who made a practice of cheating the people from whom they collected the taxes)—folks who felt a need for God and His forgiveness. They could not get what they wanted and needed from the religious leaders; these religious leaders showed disdain toward the "sinners." The religious leaders were the ruling class of Jews. They were typically the wealthy and more educated, certainly not ones to mix with the "rabble" or "common" people. That was one of their major complaints about Jesus: He not only mixed with the common people, He seemed to like it and they seemed to like Him. In contrast, the religious leaders looked upon these people as sinners who did not deserve any attention.

Instead of having the attitude of the religious leaders, Jesus associated with the common people and met their needs. They came hungry—Jesus fed them. They came sick and diseased—Jesus healed them. They came with emotional hurts—Jesus comforted them. They came as sinners—Jesus forgave them readily. They recognized that He had come from God, and Jesus showed them God's hand of love.

Those coming with the disease of leprosy—feared by all lest they also should catch it—He touched and healed. Because no one would touch or even come close to lepers, the human touch was something many probably had not felt for a long time. He was not afraid to extend that kindness and love toward them.

He defended women with reputations for immoral behavior and extended to them a hand of mercy and love. In one incident, Jesus was attending a dinner given by one of the religious leaders when a woman came in and washed His feet with her tears.[1] The woman was known for her immoral behavior and the religious leader certainly knew it. He would not have allowed the woman to touch him and judged Jesus as ungodly because He allowed the touches. Jesus had forgiven the woman, and she showed her gratitude in the most lavish way she knew.

Jesus spent time with the people. The records we have of His public ministry show that He was continually with the masses, teaching and healing. They desired to be around Him because He understood them, made time for them, and loved them. They had discovered the full manifestation of their God, and He did not act too busy or too important to be concerned with each of them. These common people were the ones to whom and for whom He came. John indicated in his gospel that only a fraction of the activities of Jesus were recorded, just enough for us to believe that Jesus is, in fact, God in the flesh.[2] Jesus apparently spent many long hours with all those who would come to Him. He healed, comforted, and taught any who wanted His touch and teaching. It appears that the public ministry of Jesus was very public indeed. By way of contrast, have you ever tried to have an audience with the president of the United States? Jesus, the most important and powerful man ever to walk this earth, spent His time with the ones most important to

Him—not those in powerful positions, but all those who recognized their own need.

And just what did Jesus do when He was with the people? He taught them. He taught them using simple stories to which they could relate. He used everyday examples and referenced events and issues that affected their lives and livelihoods. He taught them with His actions toward them. He taught them by demonstrating a love for each person regardless of particular conditions or circumstances. He taught them showing a servant's attitude. In fact, He said He came not to be served but to serve.

What Did Jesus Teach?

Jesus taught by word and example, and in the following pages we'll look at a few of His most important lessons: the servant's attitude, obedience from the heart, and the essence of true worship.

The Servant's Attitude

The disciples were arguing about who among them was the most important. They probably discussed who was second in command and who would hold the greatest position when Jesus was crowned king. They were no different and no more saintly than we are; they had to be changed and learn the servant's attitude. So Jesus put a small child in the middle of the arguing group and declared that they would need to be as simple in demand and position as the child.[3] Remember, in that time and culture a child had little value. The men were important and made the decisions. They probably felt puzzled and disturbed when they heard Jesus say, "Become as little children."[4] The child trusted simply and depended completely on the adults in his or her life.

Two of the disciples, brothers, wanted the highest places of honor in Jesus' kingdom and requested it. They were proud enough and arrogant enough to claim they could overcome whatever trouble came. Their attitude brings to mind the words of the song, *My Way*[5], popular some years ago. The theme of the song is that I can handle any problem or situation without help or advice from anyone.

Well, Jesus told them they would indeed have trouble, but He would not promise them the highest positions. Guess what? When the other disciples heard about the request, they were not happy. They all wanted the same positions. They expected competition for the few chief spots and would try all kinds of methods to get in front of the others. Kind of reminds me of corporate America.

Just before His death, Jesus was eating dinner with His disciples. He got up, gathered a basin of water and a towel, put on servant's garb, and washed the feet of His disciples—a task typically reserved for servants.[6] Jesus did this to teach a couple of lessons, one of which was the attitude of a servant. He led His disciples to recognize that although He was the most powerful among them, He served them. That was the example for them to follow. The greatest is to be the one serving others.

Actually, if we look at our true relationship to God, He is still serving us. He dressed Himself in a body (Jesus) and came to serve. He is still serving today. We often hear people say they believed the gospel message and are now serving God. Well, it is great for people to do what they feel is God's bidding, His "call." And it is important for us to want to "do" to please God, but we never should miss the full truth that even while we are serving God, He is serving us. That is an important concept to grasp.

Obedience from the Heart

Heartfelt obedience is another lesson Jesus taught. How do we obey? We obey from the heart. Do the actions always portray the heart? No!

The apostle Paul articulated this problem when he wrote to the Romans. He stated that when he would attempt to do well (things pleasing to God) the evil in his nature fought against it.[7] He wanted to obey—it was his heart's desire to obey—but that other force seemed to always fight against the good. The same is true for us today. If we Christians are honest with ourselves, we understand and have experienced the same struggle Paul explained. The heart is the place of obedience, and the heart is what we are judged by.

Because he was afraid, Peter denied that he knew Jesus three times. Was it really in Peter's heart to deny Jesus? If it was truly in his heart, why did he repent and spend the night crying? In his heart he did not want to fail. He had bragged that he was brave and promised he would not run. He failed because he was afraid, not because he wanted to. His heart was right, but his actions at that time did not follow his heart. Later, his courage returned. He was unafraid to die. He obeyed from the heart before his actions followed. It is no different with us. Faith comes to the heart first. Once the heart is turned to God, the actions will follow. We obey from the heart.

The Essence of True Worship

The Jews were taught to worship at Jerusalem in the temple, which had been rebuilt after Nebuchadnezzar destroyed it. While in Babylon, Daniel turned toward Jerusalem to pray several times each day. People made pilgrimages to Jerusalem for worship during Jesus' time. The

Scriptures tell of one pilgrimage Jesus made as an adolescent with Joseph and Mary.

But Jesus taught something different. He said people worship God with their hearts. "Worship" as used in the Scriptures is defined as adoration, reverence, paying homage.[8] Where is that actually accomplished? Must a worshipper be at a particular location? Remember, Jesus told the woman He met at the well that God desired to be worshipped in spirit and in truth.[9] As rational beings, we choose to worship God. We choose to do so because of what He has done for us.

When Jesus healed the ten lepers, one returned to worship Him.[10] Jesus was not in the temple when the healed leper came, yet the leper worshipped Jesus. Worship is not limited to a physical location (church, temple, and so forth); worship occurs in the heart and attitude. The adoration, the reverence, the homage is given regardless of our location if we are really worshipping our God.

The woman at the well talked to Jesus about the location of the place of worship. He essentially told her that true worship is in the heart. Regardless of the location and ritual, we can worship if the worship attitude is already taking place in our hearts (spirits). If the worship attitude is *not* already taking place in our hearts, no real worship will occur, regardless of the location. Therefore, instead of saying we go to a place to worship, we can say that we bring our worship to a place.

For the first several decades of the early Christian church, there were no prescribed "places of worship." Does that mean the believers did not worship? No. They met in houses, on the banks of a river, in the marketplaces, and at times even in the Jewish temple and synagogues. Cornelius worshipped in his own house.[11] If worship is adoration, reverence, and homage, we can worship anywhere and at any time.

The men who carried their paralyzed friend to Jesus but could not get into the house where Jesus was teaching climbed up on the roof, opened a hole, and lowered their friend through the roof right down in front of Jesus. Were these men worshipping by paying homage to the One who could heal their friend?

The blind beggar who learned Jesus was approaching shouted, "Jesus, You are the Son of David. You are the Messiah! Have mercy on me!" When Jesus called for the man, the man asked Jesus to heal his blindness.[12] Was that request worship? Was it paying homage or reverence to One known to be great enough to grant such a request?

Did the woman that Jesus met at the well in Samaria begin to worship when she went back to the village telling about the Messiah she had met? Was that adoration and reverence?

When the wild man out of whom Jesus cast a host of devils went back to his family and village and told of the great things God had done for him,[13] was that worship?

David committed a grievous sin, then confessed to God. His confession and prayer for mercy is recorded in the book of Psalms,[14] where he wrote (and I paraphrase), "Create a clean heart within me. Renew my spirit. Do not reject me. Do not remove Your presence from me." Was this prayer actually worship?

Our concept of worship normally focuses on the outward appearance. We think of singing songs of praise, giving prayers of thanks, raising hands, and sometimes even more demonstrative and emotional expressions as worship. Actually, these are just external outlets for the worship that happens in the heart. All of these expressions of gratitude are valid, but the true worship occurs before the external expressions. Our adoration, our reverence, and our homage are from the heart and may, therefore, produce the outward expressions.

What Was His Purpose?

So, Jesus taught that the greatest will serve. He taught that we obey from the heart. He taught us to worship. He also taught of our importance to God. In understanding our importance (or worth) to God, we need to understand His purpose. What did Jesus come to do? What was the cost to accomplish the goal? How did Jesus Himself explain the goal and our worth?

The pre-birth and birth announcements of Jesus stated that He was to save His people from their sins.[15] He was to bring salvation. The very name *Jesus* means "God's salvation." The name *Emmanuel* means "God with us." Zechariah, the father of John the Baptist, said that John would be called the prophet of the "Highest." He also called Jesus the "Dayspring from on high" and stated that Jesus would fulfill the promise given to Abraham (that all people of the earth would be blessed by this offspring of Abraham). All these announcements indicate that Jesus came to save us from sin. Jesus Himself said He came to look for and rescue those who were lost. He also knew of the crucifixion and suffering He must endure to save those who were lost. The record of His last hours before His trial and crucifixion indicates that He knew of the sufferings He would have to endure, yet He was willing to do so.

It was His purpose to free us from sin, from both its power and penalty. The only way to accomplish this was to die for our sins. Because Jesus never sinned, the Jewish leaders could find no true reason for His punishment. Thus they had to accuse Him of blasphemy, since He stated He was God's Son. Because He was guiltless, He could die in our place, granting us full forgiveness. The cost to accomplish the goal was the death of God's own Son.

Now from a business perspective, how do we arrive at the value of an item? To determine true value we find what a willing buyer will pay to a willing seller for an item when neither buyer nor seller is forced into the transaction. Our forgiveness was purchased. The price was God's Son, willingly paid. Therefore, what is our value to God?

Interestingly, Jesus gave some specific examples in a set of stories, including the stories of the farmer and the seed, the tares (weeds) and wheat (grain), the mustard seed, the leaven (yeast), the treasure in a field, the pearl of great value, and the net full of fish.[16] All of these stories give a picture of God's view of the world and us, and all have the same basic theme showing God's perspective (the kingdom of heaven). Our study will focus on two of the stories to demonstrate our worth to God.

The story of the treasure in a field tells of a man who finds a treasure, not surprisingly, in a field. He hides the treasure (not removing it from the field) and sells all he has to purchase the field. Relate that to God's view of us by asking the question, "Who gave all He had to purchase our forgiveness?" In other words, Jesus gave His life to purchase our forgiveness because He saw us as a treasure. Jesus' death purchased forgiveness for all, and the treasure is those who recognize their need and accept that forgiveness.

There was a merchant who traded in pearls. He was look-ing for fine pearls to buy and market. He found one of such great value that he sold all he had to obtain that particular pearl. Again, who paid the price for our forgiveness? Jesus gave His life to obtain the pearl of great value. From God's perspective, we were worth the price and are of great value. We are the pearl of great price.

These stories recorded from the mouth of Jesus show His willingness to give all He had—His life—to obtain us and grant forgiveness to us. What are we worth? Well, what did the willing buyer pay? You and I are worth the price of His Son given on the cross. That is God's perspective.

Chapter 7

. . . .

What Does God Expect of Me?

IN OUR STUDY so far, we have explored a heavenly perspective—what God thinks of us and how He perceives us. We learned we are important and of great value to Him, and we are able to perceive our value by the price He paid.

We have also spent some time exploring God's love for us. We learned that by definition we are loved by God's choice, not by our behavior. The examples cited from the Scriptures show the love of God being bestowed upon individuals whom we may consider undeserving. And yet, when we consider those people, we are filled with gratitude because we ourselves are also undeserving, no matter how much we would like to believe we are worthy of His love.

We also explored the area of "approval." We determined that, much like God's love, His approval of us is not based on our performance. The lives of David and Naaman helped us understand this principle.

We attempted to discover God's method of teaching. The examples given show some difficult cases and lessons, but God always seemed to take great care in teaching the lesson without destroying the student.

We also spent time trying to determine if Jesus Christ ever smiled. We looked at the evidence showing Him to have an agreeable disposition and showing that He was loved by children. We also explored His interaction with His own followers, His enemies, and people with great needs. It appears that He may have smiled, or at the very least did not appear morbid or morose.

After looking at these topics approached from God's perspective, it is now time to address the idea of responsibility: what does God expect from me?

The Expectation—What Jesus Said

A group of Jewish people came to Jesus to ask that very question. They asked what efforts they could exert, what activities they could do, to make themselves pleasing to God.[1] They were looking for the God-will-love-me-because-I-do-this formula. They were looking for the to-do list. In today's business vernacular, they wanted to build and execute the project plan. Once all the tasks were accomplished, God would be pleased. We humans want the package nice and neat and very visible.

Not only do we want it nice, neat, and visible, we want to be able to point to the completed project as our own accomplishment: "Look at what I did to make myself acceptable to God." Remember the reference to the song *My Way*? Well, the people who approached Jesus were attempting to ask how God wanted it done, but they expected to do the work themselves. Their attitude was "God, I am ready to do what You want. Let me know what deeds to perform and I will go and do them."

Jesus' answer surprised His listeners. He told them the work God expected of them was simply to believe the One God had sent. Jesus was telling them to believe on Him. The word "believe" as used in this context carries a meaning of "entrusting oneself to." In other words, Jesus was telling this group of people to entrust themselves to Him. The work, the deeds, and the effort God expended could not and cannot be accomplished by any person. It could only be accomplished by the one God-Man, God in the flesh, God incarnate, Jesus the Christ. Since He is the only One who was able to perform the task, He told the group of people to entrust themselves to Him. That was the work God expected of them—and He expects the same from us.

The Expectation—What We Want

The people struggled to accept that concept—and so do we. We human beings want to do the work ourselves. We want to build and execute the plan ourselves, and we want to be able to show our own accomplishments. It is against our nature to desire dependence on another. We want to be able to show that we did it ourselves. We want to be able to perform well enough to accomplish the work of God. We want to bring our works to Him and receive our reward in return. Jesus was declaring that we cannot. We must instead entrust ourselves, our welfare, and our acceptance with God entirely to Him.

The Pharisees in Jesus' day had an extremely difficult time with this concept. These people were proud of their heritage, proud that they were the "chosen of God." They were also proud of how well they performed their own religion. They were zealous keepers of the Law of God handed down to them from Moses. They spent large amounts of time studying that law and attempting to understand every minute detail. They fasted. They prayed. They were meticulous in giving their "payments" to the temple. They avoided contact with the "common" people and "sinners."

Jesus was not impressed. He said they performed according to the "letter of the law," but forgot the more important matters such as mercy. He explained that sin was in the heart of every individual. He told them the law had a deeper vision. While they claimed to be pure, He said they were guilty of adultery just by lusting for a woman in their hearts—even if the physical act never occurred. While they claimed they never had killed anyone, He said they were guilty of murder because they hated others. While they claimed that they were working for God, He said they were working just to be seen by others and to receive adoration from people.

Paul wrote about the Pharisees in his letters. He had been a Pharisee and therefore knew their pride and how they thought. He stated that the Pharisees attempted by their own works to establish themselves as pleasing to God. They did not entrust themselves to the One God sent, the God-Man, Jesus. They attempted to do it their own way. They wanted to demonstrate their own abilities and accomplishments. Paul indicated in his writings that they were not accepted because they did not entrust themselves to God's work.

This principle is also demonstrated even before the time of Jesus. God's basic principle is common in all of His dealings with humans. Let us revisit what happened with Naaman. He wanted to pay for his healing. He came to the prophet Elisha expecting to be commanded to perform some mighty deed or to pay a large sum. Naaman knew there was no magic in the Jordan River. He realized he was healed by the hand of God, merely because God wanted to heal him.

There was no payment, no mighty works, no real effort by Naaman; he merely had to entrust himself to the command of God from the prophet.

Moses had an idea of his calling and purpose. Yet when he first tried to free the Jews from slavery, he used his own strength and ability to kill one Egyptian overseer. Moses had to flee Egypt and spent a number of years in the wilderness before God was ready to call him again. This time he was very reluctant to go; he no longer trusted his own abilities, which is exactly what God wanted. Moses did go, and by God's work he delivered the Jews from slavery in Egypt, but he was known as a very meek man. Even when challenged and confronted by others, he did not respond. Instead, he entreated God for help and deliverance. It is interesting to see that God put Moses in circumstances that forced the Israelites to entrust themselves to him for deliverance. It was done as a picture of how we are to entrust ourselves to Jesus.

The Expectation—What God Wants

What did God expect of Adam? Remember, he committed the first sin and consequently brought all the trouble that currently exists into our world. God could have demanded a lot from him; God could have required Adam to work to attempt to rectify the evil he brought upon the world. God knew Adam was not able to perform all that was necessary, so God expected nothing from him. God planned and accomplished all that was necessary without Adam's efforts. Adam just had to entrust himself to God's efforts. He could not free even himself and certainly not all humanity from the evil his sin introduced. God provided the necessary salvation. Adam and all those who came after him are merely recipients.

Abraham was old. His wife was also old, too old to have children. God understood their age and weakness when He promised they would have a child. Not only would they have a child, but one of the descendents of that child would bless all the people of the world. How would this happen when Abraham and his wife were so old? Again, we see through this story that God performs the work, and we entrust ourselves to Him. Abraham and Sarah did have a child in their old age. That child was the father of Jacob, the father of the Jewish people. From the Jewish people was born Jesus, the One to bless all humanity.

David was anointed king even while Saul reigned. David knew his place but did not force himself to the throne. Saul tried to kill David, forcing David to run and hide. David never intended to overthrow the king and had too few followers to make the attempt even if he were so inclined. David entrusted himself to God, and God performed the work. David did not kill Saul or his family and had a relatively peaceable transition to the kingdom. God did the work in this case also.

Gideon commanded three hundred soldiers. The enemy boasted over one hundred thousand. The odds were certainly not in Gideon's favor. Yet when he blew the trumpet and his soldiers did the same, the one hundred thousand enemy soldiers turned on each other. Gideon and his men won a major victory, but in reality it was not them. It was God's work. Before the battle, God explained to Gideon that He wanted the odds to be so overwhelming that Gideon and his men could do nothing but agree that God performed the work; they could not take any credit for the victory themselves. Gideon and his soldiers just needed to entrust themselves to God's hand.

After His resurrection, Jesus asked Peter three times if he loved Him. This is an interesting account because it depicts the full story of salvation. The word Jesus used the first two times He asked the question was "God Love." He asked Peter if he loved Him as fully and deeply as God loves. The word used by Peter in each of his responses has a different meaning. Peter basically responded that he liked Jesus as a friend. The third time Jesus asked the question, He used the same word Peter used. He asked if Peter liked Him as a friend.

Jesus lowered His demand to what He knew Peter could deliver. Jesus knew that Peter could not perform the love at the same fullness and depth as God. It was God that performed for Peter. God condescended to Peter's (and our) level. God became man in Jesus Christ in order to perform what we were incapable of performing. When Jesus changed His question, it was for Peter (and us) to see that He came to meet the need of humanity.

We also see a change in Peter. Peter had come to realize that he could not perform to the same level as his God. Peter no longer expressed the pride and arrogance to say he could perform. He had come to grips with the fact that he was weak and had the propensity to fail. He would not (and knew he could not) claim that he loved to the same fullness and depth as God. We all need to come to that same realization.

The Conclusion

When the Jews came to Jesus and asked what they needed to do to please God, they wanted to know what tasks or deeds they could perform. They wanted to be able to point it out to God (and other people) once it was accomplished. Jesus told them they could not perform it. They would have to entrust themselves to Him.

In another Scripture, the writer explained this concept. He said that God's mercy is received by those who are not working to attain it; they merely entrust themselves to it.[2] Those who try to work to deserve God's mercy miss it because they are not entrusting themselves to God's work and mercy. Instead, they are depending on their own efforts. This does not mean we shouldn't work for God. Rather, it gives perspective to our work. We work because He loves us, not to receive His love or to deserve His favor. We work, but we leave the results up to Him.

As a matter of fact, we have His favor. God provided everything for us. He performed all of the work. The forgiveness, the salvation, and the favor were all accomplished by God. He provided it all. And now He serves it to us. He brings it to us, completely done and ready for our consumption. He serves it to us—and with a smile because it pleases Him to serve us. Our duty is to receive it, to entrust ourselves to Him.

When you consider God, try to picture Him serving you. He wants to. He does the serving. It is a part of His love, His commitment, and His affection for us. He does not owe it to us, but merely wants to provide it for us. That is a major attribute of His character that I think He wants us to understand. I have one last incident to share that demonstrates this love and illustrates how I think God wants us to perceive Him.

I was helping my sister and her family move from the Washington, D.C. area to Georgia, where our parents and my wife and I lived. My sister had twins, a boy and a girl, who were three or four years old at the time. While I was helping load the truck, my uncle came to pay a visit. We knew he was coming, so he was expected by my sister and the twins.

This scene is still vivid in my memory. I was standing just outside the front door when I saw my Uncle Bill drive up. I watched as he exited the car and started walking up the driveway toward the front door, but his eyes were not on me. I started taking off my gloves, so that I could shake his hand, when I heard the door open and felt a rush behind me. My uncle knelt on the cold ground (it was December) and held his arms out to my niece and nephew. He was looking for them and they came running to him yelling, "Uncle Bill! Uncle Bill!" He hugged and kissed them and talked with them for a few seconds. Then the twins ran back into the house.

It struck me at that moment that my niece and nephew were genuinely excited to see my Uncle Bill, their "grand uncle." They were expecting him and ran to greet him (and be greeted by him). He was also expecting them. That is why his eyes were not on me, but were looking past me toward the door from which the twins would come. He obviously expected this greeting from them, and prepared for it by getting on his knees to be at their level, then holding his arms out to them. He understood something about children, but I was clueless. I saw, I think for the first time that I can remember, the reaction of children, even very young children, toward an adult who thought they were important.

The twins were expecting their Uncle Bill to greet them in such a manner. He must have made it plain in their previous meetings that they were important to him and that he had time for them. They were not concerned or even cognizant of the fact that they would soon be moving seven hundred miles away. They focused on the fact that he was there to see them. They were important to and loved by him; therefore, he was important to and loved by them. They reciprocated what they had received.

While I could not assimilate nor articulate all that occurred in those few minutes approximately thirty-five years ago, I have contemplated the scene many times. It is something I recall every time I see or think of my Uncle Bill. It is also something I considered many times when raising my own daughters and when having the opportunity to be around other children. It is also something I contemplate when thinking of God.

Is God aloof, or has He come to us on our level with His arms open wide, ready for us to run to Him? He calls us His children. He has adopted us into His family. He has said that we can come to Him as to a "dear" Daddy. He tells us to come to Him and He will give us rest and peace. By adopting us, He has proved our worth and importance to Him. Jesus told His followers that they needed to be like one of the children, simple in trust. That injunction should not be lost on us.

My niece and nephew were not concerned about whether they had behaved well enough to be accepted and loved by their uncle. They simply trusted and acted as though they were accepted and loved. My uncle also demonstrated his acceptance and love to them. In the same manner, we need to simply trust and act as though God has accepted and loves us. He has demonstrated His acceptance and love.

This incident is a picture of the way I think God wants us to see Him. He is on His knees (our level) expecting us to run and greet Him. He is waiting for us. He has time for us and a desire for us to run to Him. As my uncle enjoyed the greeting he received from the twins, so God enjoys such greetings from us, His children. Run to Him. He loves it. I think He will be smiling.

Endnotes

Introduction

1. Jeremiah 32:35
2. Daniel 5
3. "Sisyphus." The Encyclopedia Britannica. 1988.
4. Exodus 1–12
5. Joshua 6:21
6. Deuteronomy 28:15–68
7. Genesis 12–17
8. Psalm 51
9. 2 Chronicles 33:1–13
10. 1 Kings 19:9–18
11. Psalm 32:8–9
12. Isaiah 41:8
13. Exodus 33:11
14. 1 Samuel 13:14; 1 Kings 11:4; 1 Kings 15:3

Chapter 1

1. Matthew 19:13–15; Mark 10:13–16; Luke 18:15–17
2. Matthew 22:15–22; Mark 12:13–17; Luke 20:20–26

3. Matthew 22:23–34; Mark 12:18–27; Luke 20:27–38
4. John 8:3–11
5. Matthew 14:25–33
6. Matthew 4:18–22; Mark 2:14; Luke 5:1–11
7. John 1:37–40

Chapter 2

1. Matthew 16:16
2. Matthew 26:69–75
3. John 21:15–17
4. Acts 2:14–36
5. Acts 3:1–6
6. Acts 9:36–42
7. Acts 10
8. Acts 7:58; 8:1; 9:1
9. Acts 9:3–20
10. 1 Timothy 1:12–15
11. Mark 9:34–37; Luke 9:46–48; Matthew 18:1–5
12. Matthew 20:25–28
13. John 13:4–5
14. Matthew 11:2–11
15. Mark 6:29–31
16. Mark 8:30–31
17. Mark 14:50
18. Luke 24:38–48
19. Luke 15:1
20. Luke 7:37–50
21. Mark 2:14–15
22. Mark 2:14–16
23. Luke 15
24. Genesis 2–3

Chapter 3

1. *Webster's Seventh New Collegiate Dictionary*
   G. & C. Merriam Company 1969.

Endnotes

2. Adamson, Andrew, Director. *Prince Caspian*. Walt Disney Pictures and Walden Media, 2008
3. John 6:28–29
4. 2 Samuel 7:11–22
5. 2 Samuel 13
6. 2 Samuel 15–19
7. 2 Samuel 11
8. Psalm 51
9. 2 Kings 5

Chapter 4

1. Strong, James. *Strong's Exhaustive Concordance*, Associated Publishers and Authors Inc., 1894.
2. *Webster's Seventh New Collegiate Dictionary* G. & C. Merriam Company 1969.
3. 1 Corinthians 13
4. Over the years I've read a number of books that convey this idea, and I have observed the idea and its converse in practice. Some of the most noteworthy books for me (though there are others) are:
Dobson, James C. *What Wives Wish Their Husbands Knew About Women*, Tyndale House Publishers, 1979.
Chapman, Gary. *The Five Love Languages*, Northfield Publishing, 1992.
5. The most enlightening book for me explaining this concept was given to me by a good friend after my first daughter was born. The friend perceived the need and the book was very helpful.
Campbell, Ross. *How to Really Love Your Child*, David C. Cook, 2004.
6. Genesis 24:67
7. 1 Samuel 25
8. Ruth
9. 2 Chronicles 33:1–13
10. Acts 9
11. Daniel 4
12. Judges 6–7

13. John 8:3–11
14. Luke 7:11–16
15. Mark 2:1–12; Luke 5:17–26
16. Mark 10:46–52
17. Acts 7:57–59
18. Acts 8:1–3
19. Acts 9:1–20
20. Luke 5:1–11
21. Mark 14:27–31
22. Luke 22:55–62
23. John 21:15–19
24. Acts 13:5–13
25. Acts 15:36–40
26. 2 Timothy 4:11
27. Job 38–42
28. 2 Samuel 11:27
29. 2 Samuel 12
30. Genesis 37
31. Genesis 39
32. Genesis 40–45
33. 1 Samuel 16–20
34. Acts 9:23
35. Philippians 4:11
36. Daniel 4
37. Genesis 25:24–28
38. Genesis 25:29–34
39. Matthew 26:75
40. Matthew 27:3–5
41. Luke 18:10–14
42. Jonah 1–4
43. Ruth 1–4
44. Acts 10–11
45. Acts 9:36–42
46. Mark 3:17
47. Mark 9:38–39
48. Luke 9:54
49. Matthew 20:20–24

Endnotes

Chapter 5

1. John 4

Chapter 6

1. Luke 7:36–50
2. John 21:25, 2 Corinthians 5:19, 1 Timothy 3:16
3. Mark 9:33–37
4. Matthew 18:3
5. Sinatra, Frank. "My Way." Hollywood, CA, 1968.
6. John 13:1–17
7. Romans 7
8. Strong, James. *Strong's Exhaustive Concordance*, Associated Publishers and Authors Inc., 1894.
9. John 4:23–24
10. Luke 17:12–16
11. Acts 10
12. Mark 10:46-52
13. Mark 5:1–20
14. Psalms 51
15. Luke 1–2
16. Matthew 13

Chapter 7

1. John 6:28–29
2. Romans 4:3–5

LaVergne, TN USA
03 November 2010
203341LV00003B/1/P